Mastering Skills for the TOEFL® iBT

Advanced　　WRITING

Mastering Skills for the TOEFL® iBT: Writing

Moraig Macgillivray • Patrick Yancey • Casey Malarcher

© 2006 Compass Publishing

Acquisitions Editor: Casey Malarcher
Development Editors: Garrett Byrne, David Charlton, Chan-hee Park
Contributing Writers: Kayang Gagiano, Eric Williamson
Recording Manager: Wendy Oh
Recording Assistant: Elisa Ha
Cover/Interior Design: Design Plus

email: info@compasspub.com
http://www.compasspub.com

ISBN: 978-1-59966-011-0

20 19 18 17 16 15 14 13 12 11 10 9 8 7 6 5 4
09 08 07

Photo Credits
• Cover ©JupiterImages Corporation
• p. 143 ©JupiterImages Corporation

Mastering Skills for the TOEFL® iBT

Advanced

Patrick Yancey · Moraig Macgillivray · Casey Malarcher

WRITING

Compass Publishing

Table of **Contents**

Introduction

What to Expect on the TOEFL® Test

The TOEFL® test (Test of English as a Foreign Language) is an Internet-based test designed to assess English proficiency in non-native speakers who want to achieve academic success as well as effective communication. Most people take the TOEFL® test to gain admission into universities and colleges where instruction is in English. Additionally, many employers, government agencies, etc. use the scores to determine a person's English ability. It is not meant to test academic knowledge or computer ability, and as such, questions are always based on materials found in the test (computer tutorials are available for those not familiar with the PC). We have designed this practice book to be as similar as possible to the actual computer-based test in format and appearance in order to better prepare you for the TOEFL® test.

The TOEFL® test, like this series, is divided into four sections: reading, listening, speaking, and writing.

Major Changes in the Internet-Based TOEFL® (iBT)

- **General**
  - ⇨ The test measures all four language skills equally; a speaking section is included.
  - ⇨ The Test of Spoken English® (TSE®) will now be part of the TOEFL® test. Test takers will no longer take the TSE® as a separate test.
  - ⇨ The order of sections in the test are as follows:

        Reading
        Listening
        (10-minute break)
        Speaking
        Writing

  - ⇨ The test is approximately four hours long and can be taken in one day.
  - ⇨ Tests are administered through the Internet in test centers around the world.
  - ⇨ Unlike past tests, there is no structure section.
  - ⇨ Note-taking is allowed in every section.
  - ⇨ The test is a linear exam, not computer adaptive; each test taker receives the same range of questions.
  - ⇨ The scores will be viewed online.

- **Reading/Listening**
  - ⇨ Passages for Reading and Listening are longer than those in the CBT (See introduction of individual sections for further details).

- **Speaking/Writing**
  - ⇨ Tasks for Speaking and Writing include integrated questions that require more than one skill to complete, i.e., reading and/or listening, then speaking or writing.
  - ⇨ For the speaking section, test takers speak into a microphone, and their responses are digitized and sent to the ETS Online Scoring Network.
  - ⇨ For the writing section, test takers must type their responses.

The New Test Format

Section	Number of Questions	Time (minutes)	Score
Reading	3–5 passages • 12–14 questions each • 700 words per passage	60–100	30 points
Listening	4–6 lectures • 6 questions each • 500–800 words (4–6 min.) 2–3 conversations • 5 questions each • 400–500 words (2–3 min.)	60–90	30 points
BREAK		10	
Speaking	2 independent tasks • 1 personal experience • 1 preference/choice 2 integrated tasks (Read-Listen-Speak) • Reading 100 words • Conversation 200 words (1–2 min.) • Lecture 200–300 words (1–2 min.) 2 integrated tasks (Listen-Speak) • Conversation 200 words (1–2 min.) • Lecture 200–300 words (1–2 min.)	20	30 points
Writing	1 independent task (same as TWE®) 1 integrated task (Read-Listen-Write) - Reading 250–300 words - Lecture 250–300 words (2 min.)	50	30 points

How this book is organized

There are four main sections and one practice test in this book.

Introduction   Understanding what each section requires you to do
Chapter 1   Practicing the basic writing skills of brainstorming, organizing, and paraphrasing
Chapter 2   Developing writing skills by connecting and supporting ideas
Chapter 3   Focusing on sentence structure and word choice
Practice Test   Practicing with questions designed according to the real test format

Test-taking and study tips

The only way to be certain of an excellent TOEFL® test score is to be able to read, write, understand, and speak English like an educated native speaker. You have no doubt been developing your ability in these areas for many years now. Unfortunately, this is not something one can accomplish by studying in the traditional way. However, research conducted over the years by applied linguists, psychologists, and educators has yielded a considerable amount of information on the best methods for refining these skills for the purposes of standardized tests. By keeping the following test-taking tips in mind, you can optimize your study habits and achieve the highest possible scores with the level of language proficiency you have developed.

General study tips:

- Prepare a study area for yourself. This should include the following:
  - ⇨ A comfortable chair and spacious table/desk
  - ⇨ Suitable lighting
  - ⇨ Good ventilation and air quality; an open window or a house plant are good ideas
  - ⇨ An area free of distractions such as outside noises/television/radio (unless of course you are using the television/radio to study listening)
  - ⇨ Proper space to keep all the materials you will need when studying, such as books, paper, pens/pencils, a tape recorder or other recording device, and if possible, a computer with Internet access

- Study regularly over a long period of time. Do not study to the point of physical/mental exhaustion, as this has been shown to be ineffective in retaining information.

- "Cramming," i.e., studying intensely for long periods before an exam, is less effective, as it strains your general health and well-being and does not lead to good long-term retention of information/skills.

- Psychologists have discovered a principle called "state-specific memory." This means you remember things better in the same conditions that you learned them. So, for example, if you always study math at night, you will do better on a math exam at night. Use this concept to your advantage. If you know when and under what conditions you will take the TOEFL® test, simulate these in your study environment and habits. For example, if you will take the TOEFL® test on a Sunday afternoon from your computer at home, then make it a point to study at this computer on Sunday afternoons.

- Be well rested on the day of the exam. Do not stay up all night studying. Also, eat healthy foods including fruits and vegetables.

- Be relaxed and confident. Do the best that you can and do not worry excessively about any mistakes or uncertainties.

Registering for the TOEFL® test

Students must get registration information for the TOEFL® test. Registration information can be obtained online at the ETS website. The Internet address is www.ets.org/toefl. The website provides information such as testing locations, costs, and identification requirements. The website also provides other test preparation material.

The registration information, such as the test center location, identification requirements, and costs, will vary depending on the country in which you take the test. Be sure to follow these requirements carefully. If you do not have the proper requirements in order, you may not be able to take the test. Remember that if you register online, you will need to have your credit card information ready.

What TOEFL® test scores can be used for

The primary use of TOEFL® test scores is for acceptance into institutions such as universities and colleges in which English is the primary language of instruction. As noted earlier in this introduction, a great number of universities and other institutions require a certain TOEFL® test score for admission. In fact, it is estimated that as many as 4,400 such institutions require TOEFL® test scores for admission.

The exact calculation of a TOEFL® test score is complicated and probably not necessary for the student to understand. It is helpful to know, however, that each section of the Internet-based test is worth the same amount of points. The highest possible score on the iBT is 120 points. Each particular institution, for example, a university, will have its own score requirements for admission. For that reason, it is very important to check with each institution individually to find out what its admission requirements are. For example, a passing score at one university may not be a passing score at another university. It is the responsibility of the student to find out what the requirements are for each institution.

Although the primary use of TOEFL® test scores is for admission into English language institutions, there are a number of other places that require TOEFL® test scores. For example, many government agencies require TOEFL® test scores to evaluate an applicant's English ability for employment. In addition, many companies and corporations worldwide may also request TOEFL® test scores for similar uses. Even language institutes may request TOEFL® test scores for use in placing students in the appropriate level of English instruction.

Certainly, doing well on the TOEFL® test is important in many ways. Remember, practice makes perfect. We hope that you will take full advantage of this practice book and study hard. Your hard work and dedication will provide you with the best opportunity to do well on the TOEFL® test and to meet your goals for the future.

Writing

The writing section of the test is designed to assess your ability to organize and support your ideas in essay format. You will have two writing tasks. One task is based on both a reading and a lecture. You will be required to summarize the information you have heard, and to relate the information heard in the lecture to the information in the passage. The second task requires you to generate an essay based on your own experience. In this second task, you will be given no material to work with; it will be based completely on your own ideas.

● **Question Types:**

Questions for the writing section of the TOEFL® test will appear in the following order:

Question	Type	Suggested Time	Response Length	Description
1	Integrated: 250-300 wd reading 250-300 wd lecture	20 minutes	150-225 wds	Contrast information presented in the reading passage with information presented in the lecture
2	Independent	30 minutes	300+ wds	Present a personal opinion or describe experience, including details and examples

Study Tips

- **Integrated Writing:**
  - ⇨ Look for magazine or newspaper articles that are about 300 words long. Time yourself as you read the articles. You should aim to read 300 words in less than three minutes. After reading, try to outline the article. Then, without looking back at the article, try to write a summary of the article from your outline.
  - ⇨ Practice listening to short reports given in English. There are many websites where such reports are available online. While you listen to a report, take notes. Try to summarize the report from your notes.
  - ⇨ Look for a variety of exercises in writing books that practice paraphrasing. Study the methods such books suggest for paraphrasing. Focus especially on exercises that practice the usage of synonyms and/or changing the grammar of given sentences in order to paraphrase them.
  - ⇨ Review useful phrases and expressions for citing sources. Pay attention to where these citation phrases can be placed in sentences and how the phrases should be punctuated.
  - ⇨ Practice your typing skills in English. You must type your essay for the TOEFL® iBT.

- **Independent Writing:**
  - ⇨ Practice writing TOEFL® essays. Get a list of sample topics at www.ets.org/Media/Tests/TOEFL/pdf/989563wt.pdf. Select a topic at random and write a 30-minute draft essay. Correct the essay, with the assistance of a teacher if possible, and rewrite it with the suggested corrections.
  - ⇨ When you are studying a group of writing topics, practice sorting them into "opinion" or "experience" topics. This will help you quickly determine the appropriate writing task you will have when you take the test.
  - ⇨ Practice outlining ideas before you write. You can do this by taking five or six topics for writing and making a short outline for each one. Don't write the essays; just write the outlines. You can also use different techniques for prewriting, such as making simple charts of information, drawing bubble diagrams, or creating lists of ideas.
  - ⇨ Look for a variety of exercises in writing books that practice writing introductions and conclusions. Study the methods that these books suggest for writing introductions and conclusions. Pay attention to tips for beginning and ending introductions and conclusions.
  - ⇨ Practice your typing skills in English. You must type your essay for the TOEFL® iBT.

Test management:

- In the integrated writing, you will read a passage and listen to a lecture afterwards. The reading passage disappears during the listening and reappears after the listening, so don't worry about taking notes about all of the key points in the reading. However, you will NOT be able to hear the listening again, so it is very important to take good notes while you listen.

- You have to type in your answers. You can use icon buttons at the top of the screen for editing. The editing tools include cut, paste, undo, and redo.

- Keep the style of essay writing in English in mind. First select a main idea, explain it clearly, then support and develop it using details and/or examples. Be sure your essay has a logical flow. There should be a reason for every sentence in your essay. Such reasons include introducing a new example or detail to support the main idea, or explaining or supporting an example or detail mentioned previously. Do not write any sentences that are unrelated to your main idea or that do not fit into the organizational structure of your essay just to increase your word count.

- Make every effort to use effective language and appropriate sentence structure and vocabulary. Try NOT to use vocabulary or constructions that you are not confident with, as these will increase your chances of making errors.

- Use a variety of language. English has a large number of synonyms and analogous constructions, so using the same construction repeatedly is considered poor style.

- Keep the 50-minute time limit for the entire writing section in mind. Remember that graders are expecting to read draft essays, not finely polished final products. If you find yourself stuck in a particular part of your essay, it is best to move on and complete the essay, then go back and fix the difficult area.

- Try to leave at least five minutes for revision. When revising, be sure to look for spelling or grammatical errors (remember, there is no spell checker on the test!) as well as ways to improve the structure and flow of your essay.

How Writing Will Be Scored

ETS graders will score test takers' essays for **integrated** writing tasks according to the following scale:

Score	General Description	Key Points
5	The essay includes important information from both the reading and the lecture and appropriately explains the information with regard to the prompt.	The essay is well organized; it may include minor errors in grammar or word choice, but the errors do not make sentences difficult to understand.
4	The essay includes most of the key points from the reading and the lecture as they relate to the prompt. Some points may not be fully explained or the explanation may be vague.	There are several minor errors with language; some ideas may not seem connected, but there are no real problems with clarity.
3	The essay has one or more of the following problems: does not include a key point from the lecture or reading, shows only a limited understanding of the information, incorrectly explains a key point, has problems with grammar or word choice that make some sentences unclear.	Errors in sentence structure and word choice may make the meaning of some sentences unclear; transitions or connections between ideas are not always easy to follow; overall, the important ideas in the essay can be understood.
2	The essay has one or more of the following problems: does not include sufficient information from the reading, lecture, or both, contains many problems with grammar or word choice so the reader cannot follow connections between ideas.	Errors in sentence structure and word choice make ideas in the essay difficult to understand in key points; readers unfamiliar with the reading and lecture may not be able to follow the essay.
1	The essay includes few or none of the key points from the reading, lecture, or both. The essay is poorly written and difficult to understand.	Frequent and serious errors in grammar and word choice make some sentences in the essay impossible to understand.
0	The essay only copies words from the prompt or is not related to the topic at all.	There is not enough of the student's writing available to score.

How Writing Will Be Scored

ETS graders will score test takers' essays for **independent** writing tasks according to the following scale:

Score	General Description	Key Points
5	The response answers the question or prompt well. The essay is easy to understand and well organized.	There is good use of language, including correct choice of words and idioms to express ideas. Minor errors in grammar and word choice are acceptable.
4	The response answers the question or prompt, but not all of the ideas are fully developed. The essay can be understood, but there are some clearly noticeable mistakes in the writing.	There is good use of language, including a variety of sentence structures and appropriate range of vocabulary. There are some minor errors in sentence structure, word form, or the use of idioms, but these errors do not make comprehension difficult.
3	The essay gives a basic answer to the question or prompt, but not many examples or details are provided. Most sentences can be understood, but errors in grammar or word choice could make the meaning of some sentences unclear.	Little use of connectors to link ideas or show progression of thought. Sentence constructions are very simple, or there are frequent errors in more complex sentence structures. Word choice and poor grammar may make some sentences vague or difficult to comprehend.
2	The essay is very short and not well organized. The ideas are not connected and examples are not explained.	Errors in grammar or word choice appear in almost every sentence. Overall, ideas are difficult to follow.
1	The essay is short and confusing. Little or no detail is given to support ideas, and irrelevant information is included. Some sentences cannot be understood by the reader.	There are serious errors in grammar and word choice.
0	The essay only copies words from the prompt or is not related to the topic at all.	Not enough of the student's writing is available to score.

Chapter 1

Thinking and Writing

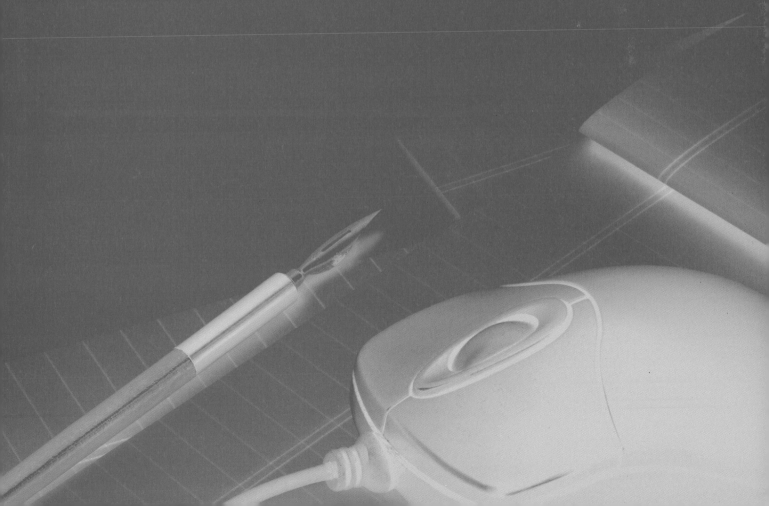

Integrated Writing: Organizing Information

Necessary Skills

- Understanding information from both reading and listening passages
- Taking notes on the reading and listening passages
- Using information from your notes in your writing
- Synthesizing the information taken from both the reading and listening passages

Process	Strategy
Read, listen, and take notes	You will not see the prompt until after you finish reading and listening, so taking notes is essential. Take notes on major points from both reading and listening.
Read the question and understand the task	Identify what kind of relationship between the reading and the listening the question asks you to discuss.
Select ideas from your notes	Choose the points that you need to discuss. Think about how the points in the lecture relate to the points in the reading. The listening passage will present details that will either challenge the information presented in the reading, present a counter example, or describe the consequences of an attempt to solve a problem presented in the reading.
Organize the ideas	Include information from both the reading and listening passages. Clearly show the relationship between the information presented in the listening and that presented in the reading passage. Limit the time for organizing to less than 2 minutes in order to give yourself more time for writing and editing.

Practice 1

Step 1

Read the following passage. Then, look at the note diagram and fill in the missing information.

Correlation studies are used to determine if two variables are related to each other. In this type of research, the researcher does not manipulate either variable, but instead measures the rates at which they occur naturally. If, for example, variable X increases in frequency as variable Y increases in frequency, X and Y are said to be positively correlated. If, on the other hand, Y decreases as X increases, X and Y are said to be negatively correlated.

For example, an investigation into the relationship between study time and grades earned might find that as the number of hours spent studying increases, exam scores also increase. This is an example of a positive correlation. An investigation into the relationship between TV time and grades earned might show a negative correlation; that is, as the number of hours spent watching TV increases, grades decrease.

Correlation studies, then, compare two or more variables and determine whether or not they have a relationship. This information is used to infer if a causal relationship exists between the variables. A causal relationship cannot always be inferred, however. For example, increased time spent watching TV may have a negative correlation with grades earned, but this does not necessarily indicate a causal relationship. It is probably the case that the more time a student spends watching TV, the less time that student will spend studying.

correlation (n):
a connection or relationship between two things

variable (n):
an aspect of an experiment that can be controlled or observed

manipulate (v):
to change; to alter

positively (adv):
in a direct relationship in which the rates of variables change in the same direction

negatively (adv):
in an inverse relationship in which the rates of variables change in opposite directions

causal (adj):
related to a cause or reason for an action

Correlation Studies: determine _____ two variables

— researchers don't _____ variables

— researchers _____ at which variables change naturally

Relationship types:

— Y increases when X increases: _____

— Y decreases when X increases: _____

— sometimes, a _____ can be inferred

Now listen to a lecture related to the topic in Step 1. Fill in the blanks of the note diagram below with the keywords or key phrases shown. Not all of the words or phrases will be used.

Main point: Correlation does _____ causation
— cannot be certain because investigators don't _____
— also, a _____ may be affecting the correlation
   ex. Eating ice cream and drowning have a _____
— but a third variable is _____

Correlations can _____ causal relationships, but more _____ is needed to prove it
   ex. A positive correlation between smoking and _____
       led to further research that proved a _____

component (n):
a part of

assess (v):
to evaluate; to analyze

validity (n):
the state of accuracy or truthfulness

vital (adj):
necessary; essential

cramp (n):
a painful tightening of a muscle

indicate (v):
to show; to state

keywords / key phrases				
negative correlation	hot weather	research	not imply	causal relationship
positive correlation	third variable	suggest	cancer	manipulate variables

Review your notes from both the reading and the lecture. Pay attention to the main ideas and supporting details. Rewrite the ideas as complete sentences.

Reading:

Main idea: _____

Supporting idea: _____

Supporting idea: _____

Lecture:

Main idea: _____

Supporting idea: _____

Supporting idea: _____

Use the main ideas and details from Steps 1, 2, and 3 to complete the passage. Include information from both the reading and the lecture.

_____ are useful tools because they describe relationships between different _____ as

they occur in the natural world. It is important, though, that researchers be careful not to make the

common erroneous assumption that a _____.

Correlations indicate when two _____ are related somehow. This implies that researchers do

not _____ either variable; they simply _____ events as they occur. For this reason, it is

_____ to determine if one variable causes the other to change.

Furthermore, there is always the possibility of a _____ causing both to change. To demonstrate,

the lecturer states that there is a positive correlation between ice cream consumption and _____.

A _____ correlation means that as one variable increases, so does the other. So, in this example,

as ice cream consumption increases, the rate of drowning _____ as well. It is a _____,

though, to interpret these findings as indicating that ice cream consumption causes drowning. In this

case, there is a third variable that is affecting both — the _____.

Sometimes, it is _____ to infer from a correlation study that one variable affects the other, such

as in the example in the reading of increased study time being correlated to _____. It is very

important, nonetheless, that one is careful to consider which _____ affects which, and that

there is not a _____ affecting changes in both variables.

Skill A Q1 History

Practice 2

Step 1

Read the following passage. Then, look at the note diagram and fill in the missing information.

Historical Revisionism is the term used to describe a re-examination of historical data. Revisionists examine and update so-called historical "facts," arguing that as societies evolve, so do their histories. These historians believe that revisionism addresses imbalances in historical narratives that have ignored or discounted certain groups in societies. They update histories by re-examining facts and including new information.

Revisionist historians argue that despite the scientific methodology of historiography, history is biased. Like any other story of the past, history is a narrative, and narratives favor the elite within societies and help them maintain power. When these power structures change, revisionism becomes necessary in order to correct imbalances perpetrated through skewed historical writing.

This idea is best understood when illustrated by an example such as the notion that Christopher Columbus discovered America. Did he really discover America? If so, what about the many indigenous peoples that had populated both American continents for thousands of years? The word "discovered" actually displays a Eurocentric bias. It implies that a part of the world only becomes "real" when Europeans know about it.

Thanks to historical revisionism, we can now qualify this notion, and consequently, in modern historical texts, quotation marks are added when the word "discovered" is used.

imbalance (n):
a lack of fairness; an inequity

discount (v):
to ignore; to not pay sufficient attention to

methodology (n):
a body of practices, procedures, and rules used by those who work in a given discipline

historiography (n):
the body of practices, procedures, and rules used by historians

perpetrate (v):
to do; to commit an unethical act

skewed (adj):
not balanced; biased

indigenous (adj):
native to an area

Issue: Historical _____: A re-_____ of historical facts

Purpose: Corrects historical _____

                    Includes new _____

Motivation: Despite scientific _____, historiography is _____

                    History is a _____ that favors the _____ in society

Example/Argument: Did Columbus _____ America?

                    No. This is a _____ bias

Now listen to a lecture related to the topic in Step 1. Fill in the blanks of the note diagram below with the keywords or key phrases shown. Not all of the words or phrases will be used.

Key Issue: Historical Revisionism has come to be used _____

Why?

— Many _____ and crackpots pose as revisionist _____

— They present badly _____ papers, books, and _____ as fact

— Their writing _____ specific events in history

— They propagate a _____ bias

This is dangerous. Why?

Non- _____ are _____ to support an inaccurate perspective

Example: Denial of the _____

Solution: Legitimate researchers must _____ this trend by producing _____ research using verifiable _____

---

pejoratively (adv): in a negative, disparaging way

tinged (adj): colored; given a certain perspective or opinion

hacks and crackpots (n phrase): people who make academic or scientific claims without any justification or proof

pose (v): to pretend to be

controversial (adj): causing many different strong emotional reactions

negate (v): to work against; to counteract

condone (v): to accept as valid

---

keywords / key phrases

political	experts	data	articles	pejoratively
researched	combat	negates	historians	methodology
imbalances	genuine	hacks	influenced	holocaust

Step 3

Review your notes from both the reading and the lecture. Pay attention to the main ideas and supporting details. Rewrite the ideas as complete sentences.

Reading:

Main idea: _____

Supporting idea: _____

Supporting idea: _____

Lecture:

Main idea: _____

Supporting idea: _____

Supporting idea: _____

Step 4

Use the main ideas and details from Steps 1, 2, and 3 above to complete the passage. Include information from both the reading and the lecture.

In the reading, historical revisionism is presented in a _____ light. The writer explains that

revisionism is an attempt to correct _____ in biased versions of the past that _____

certain groups. The writer gives the example of the _____ Americans that are ignored when

historical texts refer to Columbus as having "discovered" America. The writer believes that

_____ is necessary because as societies change, so do the power structures that govern them.

Revisionism allows historians to include _____ information and re-examine the way history is

written, so that it is told not exclusively from the perspective of the elite, _____ ruling groups

in a society.

The speaker warns us that there is a particular kind of historical revisionism that is very dangerous and

negative. This form of revisionism is often practiced by individuals with no real _____ training

or expertise. These self-proclaimed revisionists make use of _____ theories and logical

_____ in their ill-researched writing on historical subjects. Such revision also often negates or

_____ that particular historical events, such as the _____, even took place. Their

work influences non-experts negatively and gives legitimate historians a _____ name. Such

revisionism must be _____ by authentic historians who use _____ data and

supportable documentation.

Practice 3

Step 1

Read the following passage. Then, look at the note diagram and fill in the missing information.

The Big Bang theory is the most dominant scientific explanation for how our universe came into existence. This theory states that the universe was created between ten and twenty billion years ago in a cataclysmic explosion that flung matter in all directions.

This theory was first postulated as long ago as 1927 by a Belgian priest named Georges Lemaître. He argued that the entire universe had been created via the explosion of a single atom. All matter, light, and energy came from this. In 1929, the influential astronomer, Edwin Hubble, discovered experimental evidence that supported Lemaître's theory. Hubble's studies indicated that galaxies and positive space matter are travelling away from one another at speeds proportional to their distance from us. This theory, called "Hubble's Law," also implies that our universe is still expanding.

One tenet of the Big Bang theory is that the universe contains a kind of radiation called "cosmic background radiation" caused by the original explosion of the primeval atom. In 1964, scientists Robert Wilson and Arno Penzias discovered the presence of such radiation. They were awarded a Nobel Prize for their work.

dominant *(adj)*:
having the most influence or control

cataclysmic *(adj)*:
causing great damage

postulate *(v)*:
to suggest as true; to hypothesize

proportional *(adj)*:
having the same ratio

primeval *(adj)*:
having existed from the beginning; referring to the earliest times

Subject: How _____ was created.

Most _____ theory: _____ _____

Argument:

— Primeval _____ exploded, flung _____ in all _____

— All matter, _____, and energy came from this

— _____ found evidence to show universe is still _____

— "Cosmic background _____" discovered — 1964

Now listen to a lecture related to the topic in Step 1. Fill in the blanks of the note diagram below with the keywords or key phrases shown. Not all of the words or phrases will be used.

Topic: 1. _____ holes in the Big Bang theory

2. _____ theories for how the universe originated

Argument: — Big Bang evidence is too general and _____

— Evidence also supports other _____

— Big Bang never proven beyond _____ doubt

— Theory, therefore, remains _____

_____ scenario argues two parallel _____ of matter _____

Supported by same _____ data as Big Bang

Conclusion: Await new _____ via technological advances

alternative *(adj)*:
a different choice or possibility

verify *(v)*:
to check and confirm the truth of

prestigious *(adj)*:
well respected

entity *(n)*:
a thing; something that exists

empirical *(adj)*:
provable by observation, or using the senses

membrane *(n)*:
a thin layer

precision *(n)*:
the state of exactness

keywords / key phrases	hypothesis	information	vague	alternative	ekpyrotic	collided
	membranes	dominant	models	empirical	theoretical	reasonable

Review your notes from both the reading and the lecture. Pay attention to the main ideas and supporting details. Rewrite the ideas as complete sentences.

Reading:

Main idea: _____

Supporting idea: _____

Supporting idea: _____

Lecture:

Main idea: _____

Supporting idea: _____

Supporting idea: _____

Use the main ideas and details from Steps 1, 2, and 3 above to complete the passage. Include information from both the reading and the lecture.

The reading explains that there is a _____ and dominant theory about how the _____ came into existence. It is called the Big _____ theory. This theory argues that the explosion of a primeval _____, _____ of years ago, caused all light, matter, and _____ to form. The reading informs us that the Big Bang theory is _____ by Hubble's evidence indicating that the universe is _____. The theory is also supported by the discovery made by two scientists in 1964 of cosmic _____ existing in space.

The lecturer believes that there are many theoretical _____ in the Big Bang theory. Actually, the theory has never been proven true beyond a _____ doubt, and the evidence supporting it also supports other theories of how the universe may have been created. As an example, the lecturer mentions the _____ scenario. This theory argues that the universe was created when two parallel _____ of space matter _____. This theory shares many elements of the Big Bang theory but also has some _____.

Practice 4

Step 1

Read the following passage. Then, look at the note diagram and fill in the missing information.

William Shakespeare, born in Stratford around the 23rd of April, 1564, is undoubtedly the world's most famous playwright. Some scholars argue, however, that the plays accredited to him were written by someone else. They believe a nobleman who lived at approximately the same time, named Edward De Vere, the 17th Earl of Oxford, wrote Shakespeare's plays. They claim the name William Shakespeare was a pseudonym used by Oxford to disguise his identity.

The arguments that support this viewpoint are multiple: A commoner, like the real Shakespeare, would not have had the classical education that the author of his plays and sonnets displays in his writing. The real author of Shakespeare's work would also have had to be familiar with aristocratic manners and sports. Access to such information was the privilege of the nobility. Oxford was not only such a nobleman; he was a writer as well.

There is also little documentation that links Shakespeare of Stratford to the stage. Therefore, there is scant proof that he worked as an actor in London at all. The six extant examples of Shakespeare's signature are all barely legible and are also very different looking. Three of the signatures are on his will, two are on other property documents, and one is a deposition. None of them, however, appears on any play or poem.

accredit *(v)*:
to give credit for

pseudonym *(n)*:
a false name used by writers or performers

aristocratic *(adj)*:
from the ruling upper classes

documentation *(n)*:
papers that authenticate

scant *(adj)*:
little; weak; unconvincing

extant *(adj)*:
in existence

Issue: Did _____ **write the plays he is** _____ **with?**

Answer: No. Some believe the Earl of _____ did
Shakespeare is a _____

Argument:
— No _____ education
— _____ with aristocratic _____ / sports
— Oxford was nobleman and was _____
— Little documentation Shakespeare worked as _____
— Extant _____ all _____-looking, none on plays/poems

Now listen to a lecture related to the topic in Step 1. Fill in the blanks of the note diagram below with the keywords or key phrases shown. Not all of the words or phrases will be used.

Key Issue: Shakespeare _____ debate:

Some _____ believe Edward De Vere wrote Shakespeare

Argument for Shakespeare:

— Little genuine _____ evidence for Earl of _____

— It is _____, poorly- _____ conspiracy theory

— Plays not considered _____ literature: reason for no name on play texts

— Numerous _____ documents refer to Shakespeare as actor and playwright

— Why would his contemporaries help nobleman? No _____

Conclusion: _____ wrote the plays

diligently (adv):
with dedication and hard work

sketchy (adj):
not clear

conspiracy (n):
an agreement to commit an illegal or deceitful act

genuine (adj):
real; authentic

categorically (adv):
without exception or doubt; absolutely

colleague (n):
a coworker; an equal

contemporary (n):
a person living at the same time

| keywords / key phrases | Oxford | supportable | extant | playwright | researched | sketchy |
| | Shakespeare | Stratford | serious | motivation | authorship | scholars |

Step 3

Review your notes from both the reading and the lecture. Pay attention to the main ideas and supporting details. Rewrite the ideas as complete sentences.

Reading:

Main idea: _____

Supporting idea: _____

Supporting idea: _____

Lecture:

Main idea: _____

Supporting idea: _____

Supporting idea: _____

Use the main ideas and details from Steps 1, 2, and 3 above to complete the passage. Include information from both the reading and the lecture.

The reading claims that a _____ called Edward De Vere, 17th Earl of _____, actually wrote plays we accredit to William Shakespeare. He wrote them under a _____ to protect his _____. The plays _____ classical knowledge and information about aristocratic habits that Shakespeare wouldn't have been familiar with as a _____. Oxford was a nobleman with such experiences, and he was also a _____. According to the reading, there is also little documentary proof that Shakespeare worked as an actor, and his extant signatures all look _____ and, none appear on his plays or poems. All this evidence indicates that Oxford wrote Shakespeare's plays.

The speaker argues that Shakespeare did write Shakespeare. He believes that arguments favoring the Earl of Oxford are poorly _____ and states that there is a lot of _____ documentation referring to Shakespeare as an _____ and playwright. The speaker also argues that Shakespeare's name does not appear on his plays and poems because plays weren't considered important or serious _____ at that time. He believes Shakespeare's _____ had no reason to help an aristocrat like Oxford hide his true identity and that, therefore, Shakespeare did write his own plays. He thinks the theory about Oxford is a _____ theory.

Integrated Writing: Paraphrasing

Necessary Skills

- Understanding the original text accurately
- Using your own words to convey essential information and ideas from the reading and listening
- Being able to express the same information using different vocabulary and sentence structure

The Process of Paraphrasing

- Understand the full meaning of the original text.
- Take notes on the passage. Write down key information including a few phrases, major points, and important details.
- WITHOUT looking at the original passage, paraphrase the information in your own words, just by looking at your notes.
- Check the original passage for any missed key information.

Strategy

- Use related words and phrases, including synonyms and antonyms of words and concepts in the original passage.

  Example: The average daytime temperature in the Gobi desert does not often go below 38°C. → The average daytime temperature in the Gobi desert is usually at or above 38°C.

- Change word forms and rephrase to make things simpler.

  Example: for organization → in order to organize

  people at the age of thirty → thirty-year-old people

- Use different sentence structure.

  Example: Many Asian countries export rice to North America. →

  Rice is exported to North America by many Asian countries.

- Change the order of presentation of the information.
- Cite information from the original source by using signal words.

  Example: According to the professor/passage, →

  The speaker says/mentions/states/argues/believes/found that, etc.

Practice 1

Read the following passage. Underline the main idea. Predict how the listening passage may contrast with the reading.

One serious problem facing modern children is a lack of sleep. Experts claim that elementary school children should sleep nine hours each night. Studies show that children who get an inadequate amount of sleep can suffer in school and are at higher risk for accidental injury.

According to governmental agencies, about one third of all children do not get the minimum amount of sleep they require. Recent studies confirm this. After studying a group of 77 fourth and sixth-graders, Israeli psychologist Avi Sadeh reported that as little as one extra hour of sleep per night significantly improved academic performance. On tests assessing attention span and memory, students who received more sleep improved their performance by as much as two grade levels. Conversely, students who lost an hour of sleep showed no improvement on the memory and attention span tests. Indeed, on tests measuring reaction times, they performed significantly poorer than they had before being deprived of sleep.

An Italian study found that children under 14 who slept less than 10 hours a day were 86 percent more likely to be injured on the playground. Children between ages three and five who slept less than 10 hours a day also seemed to have a significant increase in injury risk. Studies such as these seem to support the old adage, "Early to bed and early to rise makes a man healthy, wealthy, and wise."

inadequate *(adj)*:
not good enough for a given purpose; insufficient

minimum *(adj)*:
related to the smallest amount necessary

confirm *(v)*:
to check the truth of

attention span *(n phrase)*:
the amount of time a person can mentally focus on a given task

conversely *(adv)*:
in contrast; in an opposite way

deprive *(v)*:
to keep from; to prevent from getting

adage *(n)*:
a brief statement of truth; an aphorism

Below is important information from the reading above. After each sentence are two possible paraphrases of it. Choose the best paraphrase for each sentence.

A. Conversely, students who lost an hour of sleep showed no improvement on the memory and attention span tests.

1. In contrast, memory and attention span tests indicated that students who slept an hour less did not improve their scores.
2. However, students who displayed no improvement on memory and attention span tests refused to lose an hour of sleep.

B. Children between ages three and five who slept less than 10 hours a day also seemed to have a significant increase in injury risk.

1. Sleeping less than 10 hours led to a rise in injuries received by young children.
2. Young children saw no significant increase in injury with less than 10 hours of sleep.

C. In the space below, write a paraphrase of the main idea that you underlined.

_____

Now listen to a lecture related to the topic in Step 1. Fill in the blanks of the note diagram below with the keywords or key phrases shown. Not all of the words or phrases will be used.

Main idea:

— sleep deprivation is _____ in poor academic performance, but not the _____

Other important factors:

— _____ (ex. breakfast) important factor

— _____ such as warm coats and shoes

— home life; ex. _____ between parents

Recommendation:

— Educators must _____ other variables before _____ more sleep to students with _____

equation *(n)*:
a consideration of all the factors that produce a result

remiss *(adj)*:
careless; negligent

prescribe *(v)*:
to assign as a means of improving health or performance

knock-down, drag-out *(adj phrase)*:
very loud or violent

vis-à-vis *(prep)*:
in relation to; regarding

psyche *(n)*:
the part of the mind responsible for one's thoughts and feelings

primary *(adj)*:
of greatest importance

keywords / key phrases				
one factor	low grades	nourishment	consider	adequate
only factor	high grades	prescribing	clothing	fighting

Step 4

Look at the phrases and sentences from the lecture notes. Try to think of synonyms for the words listed. Write correct sentences to paraphrase these notes using the synonyms that you thought of.

A. Sleep deprivation is one factor.

synonyms: deprivation - _____

factor - _____

paraphrase: _____

B. Educators must consider other variables.

synonyms: educators - _____

consider - _____

paraphrase: _____

A. Changing Keywords

Below are two incomplete paraphrases of key information from the lecture. Fill in the missing parts with words or phrases from the box. These words and phrases are synonyms or are similar in meaning to the actual words used in the lecture.

> - how much / the amount of / the quantity of
> - regarding / in relation to / concerning
> - performance / achievement / development
> - effect / ramification / significance
> - paucity / deficiency / deficit
> - greatly / largely / strongly

1. A child's _____ in school is _____ dependent on

_____ sleep he or she gets.

2. What is the _____ of a _____ of sleep _____

other factors?

B. Changing Sentence Structure

Try to complete the following paraphrases of the sentences from part A above.

1. The amount of sleep a child gets _____

2. With regard to other factors, _____?

Read the following sentences taken from the reading and the lecture. Create new sentences by combining the ideas in each pair of sentences.

1. (A) One serious problem facing modern children is a lack of sleep.

(B) Experts claim that elementary school children should sleep nine hours each night.

(A)+(B): _____

_____

_____

2. (A) Besides being well rested, children need to be well nourished.

(B) They also need to be well clothed, and, most important of all, they need a stable, loving home life.

(A)+(B): _____

_____

_____

Practice 2

Step 1

Read the following passage. Underline the main idea. Predict how the listening passage may contrast with the reading.

Throughout history, people wanting change have had a choice as to how to bring that change about. They could choose to take up arms and bring about change through violent actions, or they could choose to bring about change through civil disobedience, that is, non-violent means. An examination of history shows that non-violent means have not been as effective as violent means. Russian revolutionaries, for example, viewed non-violence as threatening to their cause. Similarly, opponents of racial oppression in the US considered non-violence unrealistic.

In Russia, Leon Trotsky argued that violence was an essential component of any revolutionary effort. In dealing with class struggle, he viewed non-violence as a way of imposing bourgeois morals and values on the proletariat. A disposition toward violent protest was, in his opinion, an essential tool for the emancipation of the proletariat. Indeed, the Russian proletariat achieved their desired change through violent upheaval.

Non-violence was also harshly criticized during racial equality movements in the US. George Jackson stated, "Non-violence is a false ideal." Malcolm X agreed with Jackson's perspective, stating, "It is criminal to teach a man not to defend himself when he is the constant victim of brutal attacks." Once again, the violent actions of these protesters helped effect the change they sought.

revolutionary (n):
a person closely involved in bringing about a revolution

oppression (n):
the act of using authority and force to deprive another group of freedoms

bourgeois (adj):
of the middle class

proletariat (n):
the working class

disposition (n):
a tendency toward a certain action or characteristic

emancipation (n):
the act of freeing people from oppression

upheaval (n):
a change or disturbance that greatly affects something

Step 2

Below is important information from the reading above. After each sentence are two possible paraphrases of it. Choose the best paraphrase for each sentence.

A. A disposition toward violent protest was, in his opinion, an essential tool for the emancipation of the proletariat.

    1. He believed that a tendency toward violent protest was an integral ingredient in the freeing of the middle class.

    2. The freeing of the middle class, he believed, was very important in the tendency toward violent protest.

B. George Jackson, stated, "Non-violence is a false ideal."

    1. George Jackson contended that non-violence was not a realistic concept.

    2. George Jackson falsely argued examples for non-violence.

C. In the space below, write a paraphrase of the main idea you underlined.

_____

Now listen to a lecture related to the topic in Step 1. Fill in the blanks of the note diagram below with the keywords or key phrases shown. Not all of the words or phrases will be used.

Key forms of non-violence are:

Civil Disobedience:

— _____ and government _____ each other

— principle of "_____" is the driving idea

— provides the _____ advantage of being _____

Passive Resistance:

— _____ break the law

— must expect to be _____ by _____

— should quietly _____ without _____

pioneer (v):
to invent something; to do some action first

boycott (v):
to not buy products from a company or country in protest

par excellence (adj phrase):
being the best or truest example; quintessential

martyr (n):
a figure respected for sacrificing him or herself for a cause

blockade (n):
a group of people or objects put in place to block the progress of something

get wind of (v phrase):
to hear about; to learn of

debilitate (v):
to injure; to damage something so that it can no longer function

keywords / key phrases	individual	authorities	resist	moral	peacefully
	attacked	don't support	retaliation	right	independence

Look at the phrases and sentences from the lecture notes. Try to think of synonyms for the words listed. Write correct sentences to paraphrase these notes using the synonyms that you thought of.

A. Principle of independence is the driving idea.

synonyms: principle - _____

independence - _____

paraphrase: _____

B. Should quietly resist without retaliation.

synonyms: resist - _____

retaliation - _____

paraphrase: _____

A. Changing Keywords

Below are two incomplete paraphrases of key information from the lecture. Fill in the missing parts with words or phrases from the box. These words and phrases are synonyms or are similar in meaning to the actual words used in the lecture.

- successfully / effectively / efficiently
- autonomy / self-determination / independence
- finish / eliminate / give up
- government / control / power
- fair / just / right
- rule to follow / principle / guideline
- using / resorting to / utilizing
- reaching / achieving / accomplishing
- convinced / influenced / swayed
- hostility / aggression / bloodshed

1. _____ in mind and action is the guiding _____ for _____ what is

   _____.

2. Without _____ to _____, Gandhi _____ _____ the English

   to _____ colonial _____ in India.

B. Changing Sentence Structure

Try to complete the following paraphrases of the sentences from part A above.

1. The guiding principle for _____

2. Gandhi effectively persuaded the _____

Read the following sentences taken from the reading and the lecture. Create new sentences by combining the ideas in each pair of sentences.

1. **(A)** Non-Violent forms of protest are ineffective.
   (B) Without resorting to violence, Gandhi effectively persuaded the English to end colonial rule in India.

   (A)+(B): _____

   _____

2. **(A)** Violence, in many ways, defines the revolutionary spirit.
   (B) Independence in mind and action is the guiding principle for achieving what is just.

   (A)+(B): _____

   _____

Practice 3

Step 1

Read the following passage. Underline the main idea. Predict how the listening passage may contrast with the reading.

> Accepted views that only carbon-based chemical systems can support life are increasingly coming under attack. Theories on alternative biochemistry suggest that non-carbon-based forms of life could be possible in unusual environments. Two proposed alternatives include silicon-based and sulfur-based forms of life.
>
> The possibility of silicon-based life as an alternative to carbon is real. The Earth is exceptionally silicon rich and carbon poor. Silicon-based life may be selected for survival in remote corners of our planet or especially in extra-terrestrial environments closer to the sun. Sulfur, like carbon, is water soluble and able to form the long molecule chains necessary for biological evolution. However, the possibilities of complex sulfur-based beings evolving are low. On the other hand, sulfur-based bacteria with metabolisms that break down hydrogen instead of oxygen have been found in exotic corners of the Earth.
>
> All suggested forms of alternative biochemistry involve odd physical conditions uncommon or non-existent on Earth. This is because odd physical conditions may actually favor these alternative types of life. Arguably, these conditions are likely to result in the formation of non-carbon-based life.

biochemistry (n):
the study of the chemicals in living things

exceptionally (adv):
in a large or intense way

extra terrestrial (adj phrase):
not on Earth

soluble (adj):
able to dissolve, or break into small particles, in water

being (n):
a living thing

arguably (adv):
it can be logically argued though not proven

Step 2

Below is important information from the reading above. After each sentence are two possible paraphrases of it. Choose the best paraphrase for each sentence.

A. Two proposed alternatives include silicon-based and sulfur-based forms of life.

1. Both silicon and sulfur-based organisms have been suggested as alternative life forms.

2. Sulfur-based forms of life are proposed as alternatives to silicon forms.

B. Arguably, these conditions are likely to result in the formation of non-carbon-based life.

1. The argument is that a non-carbon environment would probably result in carbon-based life.

2. It can be argued that non-carbon-based life could probably result from these circumstances.

C. In the space below, write a paraphrase of the main idea you underlined.

_____

Step 3

🎧 Now listen to a lecture related to the topic in Step 1. Fill in the blanks of the note diagram below with the keywords or key phrases shown. Not all of the words or phrases will be used.

The argument against "carbon chauvinism"

— term _____ views that all life is _____

— all current _____ indicate carbon is _____ to life

— _____ is all carbon based

— we aren't able to test _____

— we have no _____ data about non-carbon _____

— _____ state of science not _____ of carbon chauvinism

chauvinism (n): a prejudiced belief in the superiority of one's own group

discredit (v): to create doubt about the integrity or validity of

pre-eminent (adj): most important; most respected

abundant (adj): many; plentiful

replicate (v): to copy; to recreate

speculate (v): to theorize; to explain based on incomplete evidence

sustain (v): to maintain; to keep alive or functioning

keywords / key phrases	discredits	data	necessary	empirical	alien environments
	guilty	present	biochemistries	terrestrial life	carbon based

Step 4

Look at the phrases and sentences from the lecture notes. Try to think of synonyms for the words listed. Write correct sentences to paraphrase these notes using the synonyms that you thought of.

A. All current data indicate carbon is necessary to life.

  synonyms: data - _____

    necessary - _____

  paraphrase: _____

B. Present state of science not guilty of carbon chauvinism

  synonyms: state - _____

    guilty - _____

  paraphrase: _____

A. Changing Keywords

Below are two incomplete paraphrases of key information from the lecture. Fill in the missing parts with words or phrases from the box. These words and phrases are synonyms or are similar in meaning to the actual words used in the lecture.

- present / actual
- understand / recognize
- important / fundamental
- make-up / composition
- circumstances / environments
- proof / facts
- have / contain
- essential to / required for

1. In fact, all _____ scientific _____ indicate(s) that carbon is _____ life as we _____ it.

2. The _____ point today is that all _____ for biological life "as we know it" _____ carbon in their _____.

B. Changing Sentence Structure

Try to complete the following paraphrases of the sentences from part A above.

1. That carbon is essential to _____.

2. That all circumstances for _____.

Read the following sentences taken from the reading and the lecture. Create new sentences by combining the ideas in each pair of sentences.

1. (A) Alternative biochemistry theories suggest that non-carbon forms of life could be possible in unusual environments.

   (B) But, the reality is we can't replicate and test such alien environments.

   (A)+(B): _____

   _____

   _____

2. (A) The Earth is exceptionally silicon rich and carbon poor.

   (B) Rare carbon has proven to be the successful life base on Earth, and not abundant silicon.

   (A)+(B): _____

   _____

   _____

Practice 4

Step 1

Read the following passage. Underline the main idea. Predict how the listening passage may contrast with the reading.

Native American legal claims to the remains of Kennewick Man stand in the way of science. If kinship can be proven, these human skeletal remains will be turned over to local Native American people for a traditional reburial. If allowed to continue, further study on the Kennewick Man's remains could radically alter current theories on early migration to the Americas.

Who exactly the Kennewick Man is and where he comes from are still not clear. None of the Native American groups involved in the ownership dispute have been able to establish proof of kinship. Initial studies reveal that the remains exhibit few of the skeletal features of Native American peoples. Some anthropologists now suggest his features most closely resemble those of Polynesian peoples. If this is true, it could reveal the existence of a wave of immigration across the Pacific to the Americas. Further tests, such as DNA analysis, could provide answers to these important anthropological questions. On spiritual grounds, however, Native American groups are demanding custody of the remains and oppose more scientific study.

All studies of the remains have now been halted as the ownership dispute rages on. If Native American groups are granted ownership, any further study will be impossible. This will represent a substantial loss to scientific progress.

remains (n):
the body parts left after death

kinship (n):
a family relationship to

reburial (n):
the act of burying a dead body that has previously been buried

radically (adv):
in a large, very different way

migration (n):
the movement of people or animals in a large group

dispute (n):
an argument; a disagreement

rage on (v phrase):
to continue in an emotional or violent way

Step 2

Below is important information from the reading above. After each sentence are two possible paraphrases of it. Choose the best paraphrase for each sentence.

A. None of the Native American groups involved in the ownership dispute have been able to establish proof of kinship.

1. The Native American groups that are part of the dispute over kinship have proven their rights to ownership.

2. Of the Native American groups in the disagreement over ownership rights, none has successfully proven kinship.

B. If Native American groups are allowed to claim the Kennewick Man, any further study will be impossible.

1. Any continued examination will be impossible if Native American groups are granted custody of the Kennewick Man.

2. Native American groups will not be allowed to claim the Kennewick Man if further study is impossible.

C. In the space below, write a paraphrase of the main idea you underlined.

_____

Now listen to a lecture related to the topic in Step 1. Fill in the blanks of the note diagram below with the keywords or key phrases shown. Not all of the words or phrases will be used.

Native American claims don't mean stopping the progress of science:

— Some _____ take a _____
— Scientists argue _____ claims mean end of _____
— Native American groups not _____, just want to be consulted or involved
— Science can _____ while _____ Native American claims
— Many Native American groups involved in _____ projects
— Collaborative projects _____ and clarify scientific _____

take a hard line *(v phrase):* to leave no room for compromise when enforcing a rule or expressing an opinion

spell the end *(v phrase):* to signal the end of; to be a sign that something is about to end

accommodate *(v):* to make room for; to take into consideration

dignity *(n):* the condition of being worthy of respect

collaborative *(adj):* done by two or more people or groups

enlist *(v):* to get the help of; to recruit

enhance *(v):* to improve; to make stronger

keywords / key phrases	scientists	results	hard line	enhance	Native American
	research	respecting	anti-science	proceed	collaborative

Step 4

Look at the phrases and sentences from the lecture notes. Try to think of synonyms for the words listed. Write correct sentences to paraphrase these notes using the synonyms that you thought of.

A. Scientists argue Native American claims mean end of research

synonyms: argue - _____

                       mean - _____

paraphrase: _____

B. Science can proceed while respecting Native American claims.

synonyms: proceed - _____

                       respecting - _____

paraphrase: _____

Step 5

A. Changing Keywords

Below are two incomplete paraphrases of key information from the lecture. Fill in the missing parts with words or phrases from the box. These words and phrases are synonyms or are similar in meaning to the actual words used in the lecture.

- heart / root / core
- follow / continue / perform
- development / advancement / growth
- claims / privileges / demands
- ending / ceasing / preventing

- price / disadvantage / detriment
- traditions / beliefs / values
- remnants / vestiges / relics
- efforts / endeavors / undertakings

1. Respecting Native American _____ to archaeological _____ doesn't mean _____ the _____ of science.

2. _____ to freely _____ science at the _____ of Native American _____ are really the _____ of the debate.

B. Changing Sentence Structure

Try to complete the following paraphrases of the sentences from part A above.

1. Preventing the advancement _____.

2. The core of the conflict _____.

Step 6

Read the following sentences taken from the reading and the lecture. Create new sentences by combining the ideas in each pair of sentences.

1. **(A)** Native American legal claims to the Kennewick Man stand in the way of science.
   (B) That scientific study is impossible if Native American beliefs are honored is not true.

   (A)+(B): _____

   _____

2. **(A)** All studies of the remains are now halted as the debate rages on.
   (B) What the Kennewick Man conflict shows is more collaborative work is needed, not efforts to pursue science at all costs.

   (A)+(B): _____

   _____

Necessary Skills

- Describing a personal experience
- Expressing an opinion on an issue and supporting it with concrete examples and details
- Organizing ideas in an effective way

Process	Strategy
Read the question and understand the task	Be sure that you understand the question and what the question requires you to do.
Brainstorm	Try to take less than 5 minutes to brainstorm. Write down all the ideas you can think of to support your opinion. Think of ways to express those ideas in English. Do not try to organize these points. You will select major ideas and organize them in the next step.
Organize ideas	Select major ideas that can be developed into topics. Do NOT include ideas that are unconnected to the task or main topics. Organize so that minor ideas act to support the major ideas. Select examples that clearly support the topics.

- Your organization may look like this:

Introduction	Body	Conclusion
Restatement of the question Thesis statement	Support idea 1 + examples Support idea 2 + examples Support idea 3 + examples	Restatement of the thesis

Skill C Q2 Opinion

Practice 1

Step 1

Read the question and think about possible responses. List some ideas in the blanks.

Imagine that you have received some land to use as you wish. How would you use this land? Would you use the land to earn a profit or to preserve nature? Use specific details to explain your answer.

For Profit:
sell natural resources from the land (eg. lumber)
build real estate and sell at a profit
clear land and make a golf course

_____

_____

_____

Nature Preserve:
create a wildlife reserve
grow a small crop for personal use
plant trees and other plant life

_____

_____

_____

Step 2

Read the sample response below and underline three sentences that are central to the organization of the passage.

If I were so fortunate as to receive a piece of land, I would want to use it to do something positive that would not harm the land. Because I love plants and animals, and because I love nature, I would create a wildlife reserve. The survival of many woodland creatures is threatened because their natural habitats are being destroyed. I would want to create a place where these wild animals could live safely in a natural environment that is protected from development.

Not only would this reserve create a home for animals, it would also create an opportunity for people to see the animals in their natural habitats. I think that is much more enjoyable than seeing animals in zoos. While I would charge a small admission fee, the money would go toward the care of the animals. I would not wish to make a profit off of the wildlife reserve. It would make me happy to see the land put to good use.

Many land owners are selfish and see their land as a means of making money. They don't really care about the land; they only care about their investment. Some might sell the natural resources of the land, such as lumber. Others might build houses and develop the land in order to sell it later at a profit. Personally, if I had land handed to me for free, profit would be the last thing on my mind. I would take the opportunity to protect the land and all of the plants and animals on that land.

fortunate *(adj)*:
lucky

wildlife reserve *(n phrase)*:
an area in which animals are protected from hunting and other human dangers

woodland *(n)*:
an area with forests

habitat *(n)*:
the land in which a given species lives

admission fee *(n phrase)*:
an amount of money paid to gain access

investment *(n)*:
an amount of money spent in order to gain profits in the future

lumber *(n)*:
wood sold for construction

assuredly *(adv)*:
for sure; certainly

on one's mind *(adj phrase)*:
an idea or topic frequently thought about

Answer the following questions in relation to the thesis and topic of the response in Step 2.

1. What is the thesis statement of the essay? (Write it.)

_____

_____

2. What is the topic sentence of the body paragraph? (Write it.)

_____

_____

Answer the following questions in relation to the organization of the response in Step 2.

1. Which "side" of the prompt does this essay take?

_____

_____

2. What example does the writer give to support the thesis statement?

_____

_____

3. Does the writer present a comment or idea from the other side in the conclusion? If so, what is the comment or idea?

_____

_____

4. What is the main idea of the conclusion?

_____

_____

Read the sample response presenting another possible answer to the prompt from Step 1.

Receiving a plot of land free of charge would be an excellent opportunity to make some money. Of course, how to make the most money depends on the piece of land and its characteristics. If I were given a piece of land to use as I saw fit, I would carefully assess the land and consider all of my options.

There are many different ways to make a profit off of land. For example, if the land has a lot of trees, you could cut them down and sell the lumber. If the land doesn't have any resources that could be sold, you could develop the land. If the location is ideal, you could build a house on it and sell it to a family. An even more profitable venture would be to turn the land into a subdivision. Of course, that would depend on the size of the piece of land you were working with. Personally, I think I would try to develop the land and sell it. However, if I needed to cut down some trees in order to do that, I wouldn't object to selling them in the process.

A lot of people think that development projects like the one I am suggesting are a bad idea. They say that we humans are destroying the natural habitat of a lot of wildlife. While this is true, I don't think it would affect my decision. The way I see it, developing one more piece of land is not going to make a significant difference. In addition, if I didn't develop the land to make a profit, I'm sure someone else would once they had the opportunity.

---

plot *(n)*:
a small piece of land

free of charge *(adv phrase)*:
without costing money

see fit *(v phrase)*:
to choose; to think wise or beneficial

resource *(n)*:
a thing that can be used by people

venture *(n)*:
a business enterprise involving some risk in expectation of gain

subdivision *(n)*:
an area of real estate developed into smaller pieces for homes to be built on

---

Step 5

After studying the two sample responses, give your own opinion on the prompt. Brainstorm your own ideas below. Then, type your essay on a computer.

Brainstorming

Skill C Q2 Experience

Practice 2

Step 1

Read the question and think about your own experience. List some ideas about your experience in the blanks.

Decisions can be made quickly, or they can be made after careful thought. In your experience, are decisions made quickly better or worse than decisions made after careful thought? Use specific details and examples to support your answer.

Decisions I've made quickly:
small purchases like books and CDs
to leave a job
agreeing to get married

_____

_____

Decisions I've made after careful thought:
major purchases like my car
whether to take a job overseas
to study English in university

_____

_____

Step 2

Read the sample response below and underline three sentences that are central to the organization of the passage.

There are some types of decisions that require careful thought and other types that don't. For example, when I am at the supermarket trying to decide whether to buy orange juice or apple juice, I don't have to think very hard about it because it is not important. However, sometimes I make rash decisions about important things. When I make important decisions without thinking them through, I typically make the wrong choice. In my experience, it is always best to carefully consider my options when I make major life decisions.

Major life decisions include career choices, relationship choices, and money choices. When I was offered a job in another city, for example, I considered many factors before accepting it. I thought about the location, the salary, and the possibilities for career advancement as well as being in a new place and being away from my friends and family. In contrast, I once left a job without thinking about my decision. I was working for an insurance firm, and I became angry with my boss. Without thinking, I quit my job. A day later, I realized that I should have thought that decision through. As you can see, in my experience, major decisions that are made on the spur of the moment tend to be mistakes.

I know people who prefer to go with their instincts when they make decisions. When I was considering buying a certain car, a friend of mine asked me, "How did you feel in the car? Would you be happy driving it?" The truth was, I loved the car, but I would have been foolish to buy it because it probably wouldn't fit my needs as a student. Personally, I don't trust my instincts. I have to think about all of my important choices for a long time before I can make a final decision.

require (v):
to need

rash (adj):
without much prior consideration

major (adj):
very important; chief; principal

career advancement (n phrase):
the potential to improve one's job position

firm (n):
a company; a corporation

on the spur of the moment (adv phrase):
done suddenly, without prior consideration

instinct (n):
an inner knowledge or wisdom that is not gained from thought or experience

Step 3

Answer the following questions in relation to the thesis and topic of the response in Step 2.

1. What is the thesis statement of the essay? (Write it.)

_____

_____

2. What is the topic sentence of the body paragraph? (Write it.)

_____

_____

Step 4

Answer the following questions in relation to the organization of the response in Step 2.

1. Which "side" of the question prompt does this essay take?

_____

_____

2. What example does the writer give to support the thesis statement?

_____

_____

3. Does the writer present a comment or idea from the other side in the conclusion? If so, what is the comment or idea?

_____

_____

4. What is the main idea of the conclusion?

_____

_____

Read the sample response presenting another possible answer to the prompt from Step 1.

When making any kind of decision, whether major or minor, I prefer to trust my instincts. It's a lot faster, and, in my experience, just as wise as any decision that I spend a lot of time on. For me, in fact, the decisions that I have made on the spur of the moment have been the wisest decisions I've made. Usually, I find that when I take a lot of time to consider a decision before I make a final choice, I end up making the decision that coincides with my initial instinct anyway.

For most decisions, I believe the immediate emotional reaction is usually the correct one. One example was when I decided to go to university far from my hometown. Even though I would later receive good scholarship offers from schools closer to my friends and family, I am glad I chose to move away. In fact, after graduating, I found a great job and am still very happy here. Another example is when my husband asked me to marry him, and I said "yes" without even thinking about it. We had only been dating for a few months, but I knew we would have a happy marriage. At the time, my friends and family cautioned me to think it through, but I was confident in my immediate decision, and I was right. We have been happily married for fourteen years and we have three wonderful children.

My decision-making technique is not for everybody. Some people just aren't comfortable with a decision until they have thought it out carefully. Indeed, for some types of decisions, this might be a wiser method. However, for me and for most of my decisions, I typically go with my gut feeling. It's a lot faster, and I usually make the best decision.

coincide *(v)*:
to occur in connection with

initial *(adj)*:
early; at first

scholarship *(n)*:
an amount of money given to students to pay for tuition

caution *(v)*:
to warn against

technique *(n)*:
a method; a way of doing

gut feeling *(n phrase)*:
an impulse or motivation based on emotion and instinct rather than rational thought

Step 5

After studying the two sample responses, give your own opinion on the prompt. Brainstorm your own ideas below. Then, type your essay on a computer.

Brainstorming

Skill C Q2 Opinion

Practice 3

Step 1

Read the question and think about your own opinion. List some ideas about your opinion in the blanks.

What are the advantages and disadvantages of reading books vs watching movies? State your opinion and give specific reasons and details.

Advantages of Reading Books:

more engrossing

can learn more

more intimate experience

_____

_____

_____

Advantages of Watching Movies:

more exciting

doesn't take too long

more social experience

_____

_____

_____

Step 2

Answer the following questions about how you would organize a response to the prompt.

1. Which "side" of the prompt would your essay take? Briefly write your opinion.

   _____

   _____

2. What details would you list to support your "side" of the prompt?

   _____

   _____

3. Give one example for each detail you wrote above.

   _____

   _____

Look at the two sample responses. Of the two, which agrees more with your response? Write down any keywords and key phrases that would be useful in your answer.

Since the advent of motion pictures, the use of books for entertainment has most certainly declined. Some contend that this trend produces negative effects on the individual as well as on society at large. Others defend movie watching, claiming that it is more entertaining, more convenient, and more geared to the accelerated pace of modern life. While I do enjoy watching movies, I feel that reading books provides more advantages to the reader than watching movies provides to the audience.

In my opinion, reading books has several advantages over watching movies. To begin, reading is a much more engrossing form of entertainment. Because reading involves an active, drawn-out process, the reader becomes more connected and involved with the text. Similarly, reading is a much more intimate activity than watching a movie. Of course, reading is done alone, which makes it an intimate activity, but it goes beyond that. The reader engages and relates to the setting, events, and especially the characters in a very personal way. Because a novel cannot visually present as many details as a movie, the reader creates his or her own interpretation and vision of these details. Furthermore, because the reader spends so much time connecting to the thoughts, dreams, and feelings of the characters, those characters become a part of the reader's personal experience, almost like a friend or family member. Finally, reading has the advantage of providing a source of learning. It endows the avid reader with a familiarity with literature, vocabulary, and grammatical structures, all of which boost his or her overall mental and linguistic faculty.

As the film industry has developed and expanded over the past century, fewer and fewer people have turned to reading as a source of entertainment. In my opinion, however, reading offers several advantages that movies cannot provide. These advantages include an engrossing, intimate experience, and a means of improving one's education.

advent (n):
the invention or beginning of

motion picture (n phrase):
a movie; a film

contend (v):
to believe strongly; to argue

geared to (adj phrase):
directed at; designed for

engrossing (adj):
very interesting; able to hold one's attention

drawn-out (adj):
taking a long time

engage (v):
to interest; to involve

endow (v):
to give; to provide

avid (adj):
highly interested in

faculty (n):
an ability

Keywords / Key phrases

_____   _____   _____

_____   _____

Since the advent of motion pictures, the use of books for entertainment has most certainly declined. Some contend that this trend produces negative effects on the individual as well as on society at large. Others defend movie watching, claiming that it is more entertaining, more convenient, and more geared to the accelerated pace of modern life. While I do enjoy reading books, I feel that watching movies provides the audience with a more exciting, intense, and social form of entertainment.

In my opinion, watching movies has several advantages over reading books. To begin, movies are a much more exciting and intense form of entertainment. Because films present a series of stunning, active, and visual stimuli combined with appropriately emotive auditory stimuli, the audience is brought into the story in a much more intense fashion than reading books can produce. In a similar vein, watching a movie is far more convenient as it only takes two hours or less. In contrast, reading a novel can take weeks without providing all the intense visual and auditory stimuli. Another advantage that movies have over books is that watching a film is a social activity. Whereas people read novels in the solitude of their homes, movie-goers are part of a large audience all engaged in the same activity. This helps movie watchers relate to and interact with others. Movies provide a common social experience through which people can connect with and relate to one another.

Though some literary types bemoan and lament the popularity of the film industry as compared to the book industry, I firmly believe that movies provide many advantages to society. First, films engage the senses in a much stronger way than books can. Second, they are more convenient. Finally, watching movies helps people share social experiences.

intense (adj):
strong in emotion

stunning (adj):
impressive; causing a strong emotional response

stimulus (n):
an item or event that causes a reaction

emotive (adj):
causing an emotional response

auditory (adj):
related to sound and hearing

vein (n):
a theme; a topic

solitude (n):
the state of being alone

interact (v):
to act and react to another person or thing

bemoan (v):
to complain about

lament (v):
to feel sad and complain about

Keywords / Key phrases

_____   _____   _____

_____   _____

Which response agrees with your answer and why?

_____

_____

_____

Skill C Q2 Experience

Practice 4

Step 1

Read the question and think about your own opinion. List some ideas about your opinion in the blanks.

Some people believe that art and music programs should be cut from schools. In your experience, has taking art and music when you were in school helped your adult life? Use specific details and examples to support your answer.

Art/Music programs in schools:
— Good Experiences

- Developed my general interest in education
- Developed my creativity and imagination
- Helped me think flexibly and approach school subjects in different ways

_____

_____

_____

Art/Music programs in schools:
— Bad Experiences

- Did not teach aspects relevant to my generation
- Forced to play trumpet, I wanted to play guitar
- Took my time away from more practical studies
- My teacher was not good

_____

_____

_____

Step 2

Answer the following questions about how you would organize a response to the prompt.

1. Which "side" of the prompt would your essay take? Briefly write your opinion.

   _____

   _____

2. What details would you list to support your "side" of the prompt?

   _____

   _____

3. Give one example for each detail you wrote above.

   _____

   _____

Look at the two sample responses. Of the two, which agrees more with your response? Write down any keywords and key phrases that would be useful in your answer.

Music and art programs have been mainstays in our public school system for generations. From my experience, though, I believe that neither program develops skills that the typical student will find relevant to his or her personal artistic goals or useful when entering the real world. What's more, these programs are very expensive, diverting funds from more practical studies such as computers and information technology.

When I joined my middle school band, I was forced to play the trombone, though I really wanted to learn guitar. In fact, I later ended up taking private guitar lessons years later on my own initiative. After six weeks in the band, I quit. This was partly because I found the instructor to be a bitter, hateful person, and partly because the music he was teaching us had no relevance to my personal music tastes. We studied outdated marching songs instead of more modern genres, like rock and hip hop. Again, I would later study these musical forms on my own time and with my own money.

My middle-school band teacher once told me that all of the instruments in the band room were worth more than all the equipment in the computer lab. In retrospect, I wish the school board had used this money on computer classes instead. Today, knowledge of computers and information technology is the single greatest asset people entering the workforce can have. If I'd had computer training in public school, I wouldn't have had to spend so much of my own time and money later in life to upgrade these skills.

All things considered, the art and music programs I experienced in school offered few practical benefits to my adult life. I think the money spent on these programs would have helped me more if it had been spent on computer classes instead.

mainstay (n):
a characteristic part of something over an extended period of time

relevant (adj):
important or significant to a given topic

real world (n phrase):
the period of life after schooling in which people get jobs and start families

divert (v):
to change the direction of; to take away from

initiative (n):
a decision to act

bitter (adj):
unhappy; angry

outdated (adj):
old-fashioned; no longer useful or relevant

genre (n):
a category; a type

in retrospect (adv phrase):
thinking back, or remembering, after an event is over

upgrade (v):
to improve; to modernize

Keywords / Key phrases

_____ _____ _____

_____ _____

Art and music programs are once again in danger of being cut from our public schools. In the past, this travesty has been averted time and again because people invariably remember the importance of these programs. I personally feel that art class increased the overall enjoyment of my educational experience and helped me develop the creativity and imagination I needed to further my career as an adult.

Usually, when I recollect my school years, I recall the hours of tedious memorization spent on subjects like mathematics and history. During these classes, I often found my mind wandering to thoughts of playing outside with my friends. The teachers of these subjects inspired little interest within me to progress academically. My art teacher, on the other hand, created a classroom experience full of creativity, energy, and encouragement. These art classes functioned as an anchor for me, fostering my interest in academics, thus allowing me to master the skills necessary to survive in the adult world. It sparked my interest in education by providing me with an hour of the day to look forward to.

The two greatest skills I learned in art class were creative thinking and imagination. Developing these skills in art class taught me to think flexibly. This enabled me to approach more rigorous subjects from multiple viewpoints, thus boosting my interest in them and providing me with an integral understanding of their theory and applications.

I do not currently work as an artist, even in the general sense of a performer or writer. In fact, my job is highly mathematical. Nevertheless, I use creative thinking every day to tackle problems from different directions and apply long-term strategies to development issues. Indeed, just as the three "R's" are fundamental to every education, art must also be considered indispensable to the development of the student's mind.

travesty *(n)*:
an unfair or illogical act

avert *(v)*:
to stay away from; to avoid

invariably *(adv)*:
always; without fail

recollect *(v)*:
to remember; to recall

tedious *(adj)*:
repetitive and boring

foster *(v)*:
to promote the development of

enable *(v)*:
to allow to do; to provide the necessary conditions or skills to do

rigorous *(adj)*:
strictly accurate; precise

integral *(adj)*:
very important; necessary

indispensable *(adj)*:
necessary; essential

Keywords / Key phrases

_____   _____   _____

_____   _____

Which response agrees with your answer and why?

_____

_____

_____

Necessary Skills

- Stating your opinion or thesis clearly
- Stating clear and strong topic sentences that support the thesis

Strategy

- Make your thesis statement clear and concise.
- For your thesis, do not write, "I agree with this opinion." Restate the question when giving your opinion, such as "I agree with the statement that the government should tell people when to retire."
- Make your topic sentence a summary of all the points you will cover in the paragraph.
- Write clear topic sentences that will naturally lead into the rest of the information in the paragraph.

  Example:

  Weak topic sentence — I like dogs better than cats.

  Strong topic sentence — Having a dog as a pet is better than having a cat for three main reasons.

Skill D Q2 Thesis Statements

Step 1

Read the following questions and sample thesis statements. Underline all of the words in the questions that are also in the thesis statements.

Question 1:

> Your school has received a gift of money. What do you think is the best way for your school to spend this money? Use specific reasons and details to support your choice.

Thesis statement 1:
If my school received a gift of money, I believe the money would be best spent in hiring more teachers.

Question 2:

> Many people visit museums when they travel to new places. Describe a time that you visited a museum while traveling. Was it an enjoyable experience? Why or why not? Use specific details and examples to support your answer.

Thesis statement 2:
Because of the multitude of interesting artifacts on display, I personally found my visit to the Museum of History and Anthropology while traveling through Mexico City to be a thoroughly enjoyable experience.

Question 3:

> Do you agree or disagree with the following statement? Television has destroyed communication among friends and family. Use specific reasons and examples to support your opinion.

Thesis statement 3:
I disagree with the contention that television has destroyed communication among friends and family; in fact, I believe the opposite to be true.

Question 4:

> Plants can provide food, shelter, clothing, or medicine. Tell about one kind of plant that you have found to be important to you or the people in your country. Use specific details and examples to explain your choice.

Thesis statement 4:
Because of its many uses, including shelter and food, the maple tree is an important plant to the people of my country.

Read each of the following questions. Decide if the question asks for your experience or your opinion. Then write the thesis statement that you would use in a short essay to answer each question.

Question 1:

> It has recently been announced that a large shopping center may be built in your neighborhood. Do you support or oppose this plan? Why? Use specific reasons and details to support your answer.

Does this question ask you to explain your opinion or your experience? Select one.

opinion ☐   experience ☐

Thesis statement: _____

_____

_____

Question 2:

> Some people prefer to plan activities for their free time very carefully. Others choose not to make any plans at all for their free time. Which strategy have you found to be more beneficial in your life? Use specific details and examples to describe your experience.

Does this question ask you to explain your opinion or your experience? Select one.

opinion ☐   experience ☐

Thesis statement: _____

_____

_____

Question 3:

Some people believe that it is better for children to grow up in the countryside than in a big city. In which setting did you grow up? Tell about the positive and negative aspects you experienced growing up in that setting. Use specific details and examples to develop your essay.

Does this question ask you to explain your opinion or your experience? Select one.

opinion ☐   experience ☐

Thesis statement: _____

_____

_____

Question 4:

Is the ability to read and write more important today than in the past? Why or why not? Use specific reasons and examples to support your answer.

Does this question ask you to explain your opinion or your experience? Select one.

opinion ☐   experience ☐

Thesis statement: _____

_____

_____

Skill D Q2 Topic Sentences

Read the question and three sentences that could be used in a response to each question. One of the sentences is a thesis statement. One of the sentences is the topic sentence of the body paragraph. The other sentence is a support or example used in the body paragraph. Number the sentences as follows:

Thesis statement (1)
Topic sentence (2)
Support or Example (3)

Question 1:

> The twentieth century saw great change. What is one change that strongly affected your life? Use specific details and examples to illustrate your idea.

(   ) Having the Internet in my home allows me to communicate with people around the globe.
(   ) The advent of the Internet is one twentieth-century change that has strongly affected my life.
(   ) For instance, I send emails to friends, family, and work colleagues on a daily basis.

Question 2:

> Some people believe that a college or university education should be available to all students. Others believe that higher education should be available only to top students. Discuss these views. Which view do you agree with? Explain why.

(   ) Many people radically change their attitude and work ethic after high school, so their means of future success should not be limited by what they achieved during the high school years.
(   ) Many high school students, for example, may have difficulty earning top grades because of health or relationship issues.
(   ) In my opinion, some form of post-secondary education should be available to all students, not just top students.

Question 3:

> Many people believe that the Internet has destroyed the ability to communicate face to face. Is this belief true about your friends and family? Use specific details and examples to explain your experience.

(   ) In general, the Internet has not damaged my friends' and family's ability to communicate; however, it has negatively affected the social skills of one of my cousins.

(   ) When I was visiting his house during the holidays, he spent all of New Year's Eve alone in his room playing *Doom*.

(   ) He spends several hours each day playing online games and never comes out of his room to talk to others.

Question 4:

> Businesses should hire employees for their entire lives. Do you agree or disagree? Use specific reasons and examples to support your answer.

(   ) For instance, employees are more likely to work harder and take fewer breaks if they worry about their job status.

(   ) I disagree with the argument that businesses should hire employees for their entire lives.

(   ) Having workers who know that their employment can be terminated can help increase the company's productivity.

Step 2

Read each of the following questions. Complete the thesis statement. Then write three ideas you would use in a short essay to explain or support the thesis statement.

Question 1:

> What do you consider to be the most important room in your house? Why is this room more important to you than any other room? Use specific details and examples to support your idea.

The most important room in my house is _____.

Reason 1: _____

Reason 2: _____

Reason 3: _____

Choose one of the ideas you listed above. Rewrite the idea as a full sentence that could be used as the topic sentence of a body paragraph.

Topic sentence: _____

_____

Question 2:

> Do you agree or disagree with the following statement? Parents should physically punish their children when they misbehave. Use specific reasons and details to support your opinion.

In my opinion, parents should _____.

    Reason 1: _____

    Reason 2: _____

    Reason 3: _____

Choose one of the ideas you listed above. Rewrite the idea as a full sentence that could be used as the topic sentence of a body paragraph.

Topic sentence: _____

_____

Question 3:

> There are many reasons to work, including the need for money. Describe your reasons for choosing a job that you have had or would like to have. Use specific examples and details to support your answer.

I chose my current job for _____.

    Reason 1: _____

    Reason 2: _____

    Reason 3: _____

Choose one of the ideas you listed above. Rewrite the idea as a full sentence that could be used as the topic sentence of a body paragraph.

Topic sentence: _____

_____

Question 4:

> Schools should ask students to evaluate their teachers. Do you agree or disagree? Use specific reasons and examples to support your answer.

In my opinion, asking students to evaluate their teachers is _____.

    Reason 1: _____

    Reason 2: _____

    Reason 3: _____

Choose one of the ideas you listed above. Rewrite the idea as a full sentence that could be used as the topic sentence of a body paragraph.

Topic sentence: _____

_____

Vocabulary Review

Vocabulary Review 1

Instructions: Choose the best word or phrase to complete each sentence.

1. Scientists have to control many _____ in order to conduct an accurate experiment.
   - (A) cramps
   - (B) variables
   - (C) adages
   - (D) membranes

2. The politician _____ many crimes and dishonest acts before the people finally voted him out.
   - (A) discounted
   - (B) assessed
   - (C) manipulated
   - (D) perpetrated

3. Is this species of plant _____ to this area, or was it brought in from Europe?
   - (A) indigenous
   - (B) controversial
   - (C) primeval
   - (D) prestigious

4. Many scientists believe a(n) _____ event, probably a meteor strike, caused a great environmental change that led to the extinction of dinosaurs.
   - (A) cataclysmic
   - (B) empirical
   - (C) aristocratic
   - (D) soluble

5. She wrote under a _____ because women were not believed to be capable of producing worthy literature at the time.
   - (A) precision
   - (B) conspiracy
   - (C) colleague
   - (D) pseudonym

6. My professor said my research was _____. Therefore, I have to do the paper again in order to pass the course.
   - (A) bourgeois
   - (B) abundant
   - (C) inadequate
   - (D) fortunate

7. Her doctor _____ her a list of exercises and dietary changes to help her have more energy.
   - (A) confirmed
   - (B) debilitated
   - (C) prescribed
   - (D) sustained

8. The scientists from that university tried to _____ the work of scientists from my university, but the opposite happened. They validated their results instead.
   - (A) replicate
   - (B) pioneer
   - (C) accredit
   - (D) discredit

Instructions: Choose the word or phrase closest in meaning to the underlined part.

9. The term paper is the most important <u>part</u> of your grade for this course.
   - (A) component
   - (B) correlation
   - (C) imbalance
   - (D) methodology

10. It is <u>very important</u> that governments try to fight oppression in other places around the world.
   - (A) vital
   - (B) causal
   - (C) skewed
   - (D) proportional

11. Darwin <u>theorized</u> that animals evolve to adapt to new environments.
    - (A) posed
    - (B) verified
    - (C) postulated
    - (D) deprived

12. I can't <u>accept</u> your idea to cheat on the exam.
    - (A) condone
    - (B) confirm
    - (C) prescribe
    - (D) replicate

13. The Renaissance was an <u>extremely</u> interesting period of European history.
    - (A) arguably
    - (B) exceptionally
    - (C) pejoratively
    - (D) categorically

14. We have a <u>plentiful</u> supply of food for the picnic. Why don't you join us?
    - (A) primary
    - (B) inadequate
    - (C) vital
    - (D) abundant

15. Her father attended a <u>highly respected</u> university. She's going to attend the same school next year.
    - (A) genuine
    - (B) sketchy
    - (C) prestigious
    - (D) remiss

Instructions: Write the missing words. Use the words below to fill in the blanks.

precision	verify	membranes
postulated	empirical	

An idea that has recently been **(16)** _____ is called the ekpyrotic scenario. This theory argues that our universe was created when two thin layers or **(17)** _____ of space matter collided. While this theory has some elements in common with the Big Bang Theory, it also has many differences. In fact, the ekpyrotic scenario is supported by the same **(18)** _____ data gathered from experiments designed to **(19)** _____ the Big Bang Theory. At this point, scientists must continue to investigate the subject with care and **(20)** _____. Perhaps such carefully obtained data will one day prove how the universe came into being.

Instructions: Match the words that are opposites.

21. proletariat   (A) oppression
22. inadequate   (B) balanced
23. emancipation   (C) abundant
24. confirm   (D) aristocratic
25. skewed   (E) discredit

Vocabulary Review 2

Instructions: Choose the best word or phrase to complete each sentence.

1. The Native Americans living in the area today claim a _____ to the people who lived here thousands of years ago, though it is difficult to prove they are from the same family line.
   - (A) migration
   - (B) stimulus
   - (C) lumber
   - (D) kinship

2. I believe that all people should be treated with _____ until they prove they are not worthy of respect.
   - (A) dignity
   - (B) investment
   - (C) instinct
   - (D) solitude

3. The _____ of the flying squirrel is being destroyed by the expansion of cities.
   - (A) mainstay
   - (B) genre
   - (C) travesty
   - (D) habitat

4. I'm thinking about investing in a new business _____, but I'm not sure that the risks are worth the potential profits.
   - (A) advent
   - (B) faculty
   - (C) dispute
   - (D) venture

5. My _____ impression of the professor was not very positive, but now I look forward to her classes every day.
   - (A) initial
   - (B) avid
   - (C) emotive
   - (D) auditory

6. The _____ of the radio radically changed the way people communicated in the 20th century.
   - (A) faculty
   - (B) stimulus
   - (C) advent
   - (D) vein

7. The Rocky Mountains provide tourists with some truly _____ scenery. I recommend you visit them some day.
   - (A) relevant
   - (B) stunning
   - (C) outdated
   - (D) rigorous

8. That reporter has been a _____ on the 6:00 news for thirty years.
   - (A) mainstay
   - (B) travesty
   - (C) technique
   - (D) firm

Instructions: Choose the word or phrase closest in meaning to the underlined part.

9. We are <u>lucky</u> to live in a time when global communication is so readily available.
   - (A) collaborative
   - (B) fortunate
   - (C) rash
   - (D) initial

10. The armed forces need to <u>recruit</u> hundreds of soldiers each year for their military operations abroad.
    - (A) enhance
    - (B) require
    - (C) endow
    - (D) enlist

11. I believe in following my <u>gut feelings</u> when making a difficult decision.
    - (A) solitudes
    - (B) initiatives
    - (C) instincts
    - (D) subdivisions

12. The United Nations will attempt to solve the <u>disagreement</u> between the two countries.
    - (A) dispute
    - (B) migration
    - (C) dignity
    - (D) investment

13. The airline company is going to spend more money on food and comfortable seats in order to <u>improve</u> the in-flight experience for passengers.
    - (A) enhance
    - (B) accommodate
    - (C) engage
    - (D) coincide

14. That was a very <u>interesting</u> film. I want to see it again.
    - (A) avid
    - (B) emotive
    - (C) engrossing
    - (D) stunning

15. She was very <u>unhappy</u> about spending a lot of time and money on the course, only to receive a failing grade from the professor.
    - (A) tedious
    - (B) bitter
    - (C) integral
    - (D) auditory

Instructions: Write the missing words. Use the words below to fill in the blanks.

collaborative	invariably	contend
interacting	foster	

Last year, more than fifty Native American groups were **(16)** _____ with scholars on joint archaeological programs. To be sure, such **(17)** _____ work between scientists and Native American leaders is important. It shows the possibility for scientific progress not only to learn about the past, but to **(18)** _____ respect and positive feelings between the two groups in the present. Scientists involved in these programs **(19)** _____ report numerous advantages to conducting research with the participation of Native Americans. They **(20)** _____ that a deeper understanding of the scientific data is obtained.

Instructions: Choose the one word that does not belong.

21.	vital	initial	integral	indispensable
22.	endow	bemoan	lament	complain
23.	recall	recollect	require	remember
24.	plot	woodland	habitat	technique
25.	update	caution	improve	enhance

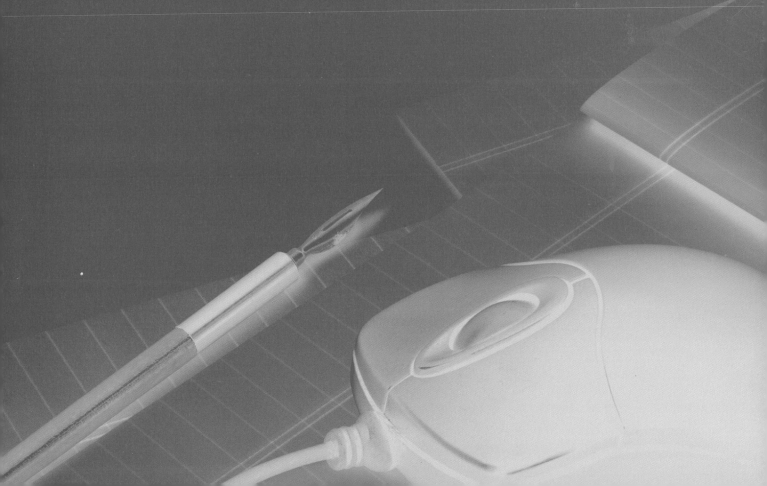

Chapter 2

Making Writing Complete

Strategies

- After determining the framework of your essay, further consideration must be given to the organization within the paragraphs themselves.

First paragraph contains:	Supporting paragraphs contain:
• the main idea of the whole response • one key point • examples and/or connection to the reading	• additional key points • examples and/or connection to the reading

- When developing your points, make sure that the statements are well connected so that the relationships between ideas can be seen clearly.
- Use transitional words and phrases to indicate the relationships among ideas.
- Use appropriate expressions to indicate when citing the source.

To Cite Information

- According to the lecture/passage,
- The reading states that
- In the reading, the author states that/discusses how
- In the author's/professor's opinion,
- According to the theory in the reading/lecture,
- The professor makes the point that
- The lecture supports/illustrates the idea that
- The lecture contradicts/refutes the idea that

To Compare and Contrast

- similarly, likewise, also, just as, both, by, by comparison, compared to, but, yet, although, in contrast, on the contrary, contrary to, on the other hand, however, conversely, is the opposite of, while, whereas, nevertheless, although, meanwhile, after all, although this may be true, in spite of, despite

To Show Cause and Effect

- because, since, for, thus, therefore, hence, as a result, accordingly, for the same reason

Practice 1

Step 1

Read the passage below and underline important information.

When most people think of great military strategists, the names Alexander the Great, Julius Caesar, or Napoleon Bonaparte come to mind. Spanish Conquistador Hernando Cortes, however, accomplished a feat that, arguably, outshines them all. Around 1520, Cortes conquered the 5-million-strong Aztec empire with only 600 men, twenty horses, and ten small cannons.

In 1519, Cortes sailed from Spain to Mexico with 11 ships and landed at various points along the Mexican coast. He easily subdued the small coastal tribes at what are now Tabasco and Veracruz. These people told him of the vast wealth of the Aztecs who lived inland. Cortes began to enlist the support of the smaller tribes he conquered as he made his way inland, a strategy that would serve him well. Since many of the tribes had no love for the Aztecs due to the Aztec policy of demanding costly tribute from them, they were often willing to join forces with Cortes.

Another circumstance that Cortes exploited was the fact that the Aztecs had a legend of a pale-skinned, bearded god, Quetzalcoatl, who they believed had once taught them agriculture and who would one day return to end their civilization. Cortes was believed to be this god by some Aztec citizens, most notably, the emperor Motecuhzoma. Additionally, the native Mexicans had never before seen horses, firearms, or the giant attack mastiffs the Spanish brought with them. Cortes exploited these two psychological advantages, the legend of the light-skinned god and the spectacle of his horses, dogs, and cannons, to conquer the entire Aztec empire largely through fear and negotiation. The brilliance of his approach leaves its mark, for better or worse, on the history of an entire nation today.

strategist (n):
a person who makes plans and strategies

come to mind (v phrase):
to be thought of

feat (n):
an accomplishment

outshine (v):
to appear or perform better than

subdue (v):
to capture and control

tribute (n):
a payment of money or goods demanded by the head of an empire from the nations under its control

firearm (n):
a gun

mastiff (n):
a large, powerful breed of dog

spectacle (n):
a large public performance or display

Step 2

🎧 **Now listen to a lecture and take notes on the important information.**

_____ was the secret to _____ 's success

1. Spaniards discover that she can _____ and use her

   _____

2. Cortes uses her to win _____ from _____

3. Unclear whether she was just an _____ or _____ as well

4. Independent _____ and _____ sources attest to

   _____

lingua franca (n phrase):
a second language spoken by people of many nations

entourage (n):
a group of people that accompany someone

concubine (n):
a woman responsible for bearing children to a man

campaign (n):
a military venture

cast doubt on (v phrase):
to make uncertain or doubtful

hierarchical (adj):
related to a ranking based on power or authority

Step 3

Read the question and understand your task.

Summarize the main points in the lecture, explaining how they cast doubt on points made in the reading.

Now read the passage and your notes again. Write down the parts of the reading and the lecture that disagree.

Reading	Lecture
_____	_____
_____	_____
_____	_____

Step 4

Read the sample response below. Identify the role of each statement and fill in the blanks with the appropriate words in the box.

The reading passage depicts Cortes as one of the greatest military strategists of all time and credits him with toppling an empire of millions with only 600 men and a few horses and cannons. **(1)** _____, it proposes he was a genius who exploited local politics, legends, and the spectacle of his small but advanced military to accomplish a nearly impossible feat. **(2)** _____, the speaker casts doubt on this version of history and credits Cortes's interpreter and concubine, Malintzin, as being the mastermind behind a significant part of his campaign. **(3)** _____, she asks us to ponder who was more likely the mastermind: the foreigner who had little to no knowledge of the politics, customs, or language, or the native who had knowledge of all of these and who was the one directly speaking with the leaders of the Aztecs and other nations. **(4)** _____, the speaker cites various sources, including accounts from Spanish soldiers and other conquistadors, as well as depictions in Nahua art, which support the case that Malintzin was much more than an interpreter and perhaps just as significant as Cortes himself.

in contrast / in addition to this / further / more specifically

Underline the main point, the example, and the final summary statement in the sample response. Then, change those sentences using your own words. Try to make your sentences as short and clear as possible.

Main Point: _____

Example Sentence: _____

Summary Sentence: _____

Step 5

Write your own response with the help of the sample and the words/phrases you wrote in Step 4.

Response word count: _____ (Suggested word count = 200)

Practice 2

Step 1

Read the passage below and underline important information.

The value of a professional sports team for a city's local economy is undeniable. The benefits begin with the construction of the stadium itself, providing thousands of local construction jobs. Once regular season play begins, an army of local workers is required to man the stadium facilities, for everything from concessions and ticket sales to security and administration. The economic benefits expand throughout the district of the stadium as fans pour into the area from far and wide. These fans support local parking decks, restaurants, bars, shops, and often hotel facilities. This contributes to the prosperity of local businesses and provides a general boost to the overall property value.

All of this revenue is of course taxed by the municipal authorities. Combine this with the millions of dollars in tax revenue that ticket sales can generate over the life of a sports team, and we have a clear benefit for all members of the community.

These benefits are easy to see, but the intangible benefits may be greater still. A professional sports team with regularly televised broadcasts is often the hallmark of what people generally perceive as a "major" city. Thus, the sports team becomes a kind of advertisement for the significance and prosperity of the city itself, attracting new business from the outside.

Some may say that the costs of new sports stadiums are an undue burden on cities, but all of the long-term benefits must be taken into account before passing hasty judgment on the economic effects of professional sports franchises.

concessions (n): the food and drink sold in a stadium

prosperity (n): the state of being successful

municipal (adj): related to a city or town

intangible (adj): not detectable by the physical senses

hallmark (n): a characteristic sign of

undue (adj): unnecessary; unjust; unwarranted

burden (n): a source of stress or difficulty

hasty (adj): done quickly, without careful consideration

Step 2

🎧 **Now listen to a lecture and take notes on the important information.**

Sports stadium not _____

1. Jobs created _____ other jobs or _____ wages

2. Most money goes to _____

3. Tax revenue _____ compared to _____

4. Team's _____ to the city's _____ difficult to measure

federal (adj): related to a nation

exempt (adj): not applicable to; an exception to

infrastructure (n): the structures necessary for a society to run smoothly, such as roads, schools, and hospitals

meager (adj): small; insufficient

feasible (adj): possible; able to be accomplished; plausible

top notch (adj phrase): of high quality or level

Read the question and understand your task.

Summarize the main points made in the lecture, explaining how they cast doubt on points made in the reading.

Now read the passage and your notes again. Write down the parts of the reading and the lecture that disagree.

Reading	Lecture
_____	_____
_____	_____
_____	_____

Step 4

Now read the sample response below. Identify the role of each statement and fill in the blanks with the appropriate words in the box.

The reading states that a sports team greatly benefits a city in a number of ways, **(1)** _____ the lecture says the benefits do not justify the initial investment and that the sports team actually ends up taking money out of the community. The speaker implies that taxpayer money should not go to the stadium **(2)** _____ the sports team is a profit-seeking business, and they should not expect free money from the public. Further, the speaker argues that benefits such as jobs and tax revenues are not actually benefits if all relevant factors are taken into account, such as the kinds of jobs, and the comparison of the situation without the sports team. **(3)** _____, the reading proposes that the benefit to the city's image is invaluable, ultimately attracting new residents and businesses and contributing to the city's long-term growth. **(4)** _____ this fact, the speaker maintains that the city would benefit more from investing this money elsewhere, such as in education and infrastructure.

since / while / in spite of / however

Underline the main point, the example, and the final summary statement in the sample response. Then, change those sentences using your own words. Try to make your sentences as short and clear as possible.

Main Point: _____

Example Sentence: _____

Summary Sentence: _____

Write your own response with the help of the sample and the words/phrases you wrote in Step 4.

Response word count: _____ (Suggested word count = 200)

Practice 3

Step 1

Read the passage below and underline important information.

In 1989, scientists in Utah made a controversial announcement. They claimed that they had carried out an experiment in which the results could only be explained by nuclear fusion. In their experiment, they filled a glass container with heavy water that had a small amount of salt dissolved in it. Into the container, they inserted two electrodes: one was platinum and one was palladium. The platinum electrode was connected to the positive charge of a car battery, while the palladium electrode was attached to the negative charge. This process created an excess amount of heat—more than could be explained by chemical reactions. Because it could not be explained by chemical reactions, the researchers jumped to the conclusion that nuclear fusion was the cause. This phenomenon is referred to as "cold fusion." It is not accepted by the scientific community, and it serves as an example of pseudoscience.

The scientific method demands that a claim be subject to peer review. The validity of any claim is based on reproducibility. Because no one has ever been able to reproduce the results of the first claim of cold fusion, it has been rejected. More importantly, the data does not coincide with current theories of nuclear fusion. It is well accepted that, when nuclear fusion takes place, neutrons are emitted. For one thing, no extra neutrons were detected. Secondly, if the number of neutrons necessary to support their claim had in fact been emitted, the researchers would have been killed. The only explanation for the experimenters' findings is that errors in measurement took place. This is supported by the fact that the methods they used to measure heat were highly specious.

carry out *(v phrase):*
to do; to perform

phenomenon *(n):*
an event; a happening

pseudoscience *(n):*
a false science; an unfounded claim of a scientific procedure

peer review *(n phrase):*
the process of having equals examine an academic work

reproducibility *(n):*
the ability to be repeated with the same results

emit *(v):*
to produce and give off

take place *(v phrase):*
to happen; to occur

specious *(adj):*
seeming to be true but actually false; deceptively attractive

Step 2

🎧 **Now listen to a lecture and take notes on the important information.**

• Cold fusion refers to _____

— _____

— _____

— _____

disdain *(n):*
a feeling of contempt for; a feeling of superiority in regards to

astound *(v):*
to surprise greatly

buy into *(v phrase):*
to believe

validate *(v):*
to prove true

deem *(v):*
to conclude; to state as

stance *(n):*
an opinion; a point of view

Step 3

Read the question and understand your task.

Summarize the main points made in the lecture, explaining how they relate to points made in the reading.

Now read the passage and your notes again. Write down the main points of the reading and the parts of the lecture that expand upon the points made in the reading.

Reading	Lecture
_____	_____
_____	_____
_____	_____

Step 4

Now read the sample response below. Identify the role of each statement and fill in the blanks with the appropriate words in the box.

The debate surrounding the possibility of cold fusion, **(1)** _____, nuclear fusion occurring at room temperature, is centered on the scientific process. The reading attacks the scientists' interpretation of their results. When they found that excess heat was generated in an amount that could not be explained by chemical reactions, the scientists concluded that nuclear fusion was taking place. The reading states that because such an interpretation does not concur with current theory, it should not be accepted. The speaker points out, however, that science relies on continual review of theories. Observations should not be ignored **(2)** _____ they are not explained by current theories. **(3)** _____ the statement in the reading that scientists have never been able to replicate the original experimenters' results, the speaker states that in the years that have passed, some indeed have found similar results. In sum, the reading states that cold fusion claims have not stood up to the scientific process, **(4)** _____ the speaker asserts that the scientific community was hasty in dismissing the notion before sufficient time was allowed to complete an analysis using the scientific process.

whereas / just because / that is / with regards to

Underline the main point, the example, and the final summary statement in the sample response. Then, change those sentences using your own words. Try to make your sentences as short and clear as possible.

Main Point: _____

Example Sentence: _____

Summary Sentence: _____

Step 5

Write your own response with the help of the sample and the words/phrases you wrote in Step 4.

Response word count: _____ (Suggested word count = 200)

Practice 4

Step 1

Read the passage below and underline important information.

Recent claims that the ancient Anasazi peoples engaged in cannibalism are unfounded. The practice of cannibalism does not coincide with the culture of the Native American groups who are descended from these people, that is, the Pueblo peoples of the American Southwest. Cannibalism is considered by Native Americans to be one of the most evil acts a person can engage in. It seems improbable, then, that their ancestors ate human flesh ritualistically. The speculation that the Anasazi people were human flesh eaters is based on skeletal remains that were found to have been broken and burned. It can be demonstrated from these findings that flesh was removed from the bones, but that does not prove that the meat was actually ingested. A more plausible explanation, and one that coincides with the beliefs of the Pueblo peoples, is that these are the remains of suspected witches who were put to death. The custom was to kill the suspected witch by burning the body and tearing apart the remains in order to remove and destroy the witch's "evil heart." This explains the broken bones and burn marks. It also explains why the corpse was ripped apart. While the practice was brutal, it does not imply cannibalism. Any claim that the Anasazi people were cannibalistic is based not on fact, but on inference. The refusal of some to consider other plausible explanations is unscientific and irrational.

engage in *(v phrase):*
to do

unfounded *(adj):*
not supported by evidence

ancestor *(n):*
a relative that lived in the past; a person whom one is descended from

ritualistically *(adv):*
as part of a ceremony or ritual

ingest *(v):*
to eat; to consume

plausible *(adj):*
possible; able to be accomplished; feasible

brutal *(adj):*
violent; extremely harsh or cruel

Step 2

🎧 **Now listen to a lecture and take notes on the important information.**

• Evidence supports the claim that _____

_____

— _____

— _____

— _____

touchy *(adj):*
causing strong emotions

revere *(v):*
to respect greatly

tag marker *(n phrase):*
a characteristic sign of

carcass *(n):*
a dead body

condemn *(v):*
to censure; to conclude as unethical or unworthy

tarnish *(v):*
to spoil; to lessen the value or purity of

Read the question and understand your task.

Summarize the points made in the lecture and state how they can be applied to the problem introduced in the reading passage.

Now read the passage and your notes again. Write down the main points of the reading and the parts of the lecture that expand upon the points made in the reading.

Reading	Lecture
_____	_____
_____	_____
_____	_____

Step 4

Now read the sample response below. Identify the role of each statement and fill in the blanks with the appropriate words in the box.

The dispute concerning whether or not the Anasazi people engaged in cannibalism is based on evidence obtained from the examination of human remains. These remains show that human skeletons were torn apart, cooked, and had the flesh removed from them. The reading states that this does not necessarily imply that cannibalism took place. **(1)** _____, they explain that these are the remains of suspected witches who were burned and had their bodies torn apart. The speaker, however, maintains that the evidence does suggest that ingestion took place. **(2)** _____, pot resin was found on the bones suggesting they were cooked. **(3)** _____, fossilized fecal matter shows traces of human flesh. While the reading states that Native American culture would not condone such activities, the speaker maintains that the evidence does not implicate anyone in particular in the act. She goes on to offer a plausible explanation that has been presented: that a group of foreigners engaged in cannibalism in order to terrorize the Anasazi. **(4)** _____, the peaceful reputation of this culture need not be tarnished by this evidence of cannibalism.

furthermore / thus / for example / instead

Underline the main point, the example, and the final summary statement in the sample response. Then, change those sentences using your own words. Try to make your sentences as short and clear as possible.

Main Point: _____

Example Sentence: _____

Summary Sentence: _____

Step 5

Write your own response with the help of the sample and the words/phrases you wrote in Step 4.

Response word count: _____ (Suggested word count = 200)

Strategies

Characteristics of a good introduction:

- is one (1) paragraph
- is an introduction to the general topic of the essay
- includes the thesis statement and a restatement of the question
- includes points that will be discussed or elaborated on in the body

- Do NOT try to say everything in the introduction; save details and examples for the body of your essay.
- Do NOT start with a statement that is too general; a more specific statement better sets up the information to follow.

Characteristics of a good body:

- can be several (1–3) paragraphs
- has a topic sentence for each paragraph that states the main idea of that paragraph
- has specific examples, reasons, or other details
- includes other sentences that link ideas or show transitions between ideas

- Write an accurate and clear topic sentence for each body paragraph.
- Make sure there are logical connections between statements.

Characteristics of a good conclusion:

- is one (1) paragraph
- has a restatement of your thesis in different words
- has a summary of your main points
- includes one or both of the following: a consideration of the opposite opinion, a recommendation

- Do NOT use the exact same words or expressions in your conclusion that you used in your introduction.
- Do NOT introduce new ideas or concepts that should belong in a new body paragraph.

Skill B Independent

Practice 1

Step 1

Read the question and think of ideas to list in the blanks.

A gift (such as a camera, a soccer ball, or an animal) can contribute to a child's development. Some gifts produce positive effects on this development, while other gifts produce negative effects. What gift that you received as a child helped you develop into the person you are today? How? Use specific details and examples to describe your experience.

Gift: Produced positive development

- Books: Stimulate the imagination
        Develop language skills such as grammar, vocabulary, etc
        Encourage creativity
        Good for relaxation and de-stressing

_____

_____

Gift: Produced negative development

- Playstation: Very competitive
        Lack of exercise due to indoor activity
        Can make children antisocial and obsessive

_____

_____

Now look at the sample response. Think of the role of sentences in each part of the essay. Look for any transitions that link the ideas and underline them. Then, put the sentences in the right order.

Introduction:

_____   _____   _____   _____

(A) It is thus, perhaps, no surprise that I ended up studying literature and finally became a language teacher and creative writer myself.
(B) Receiving my first storybook at the age of six was to change the course of my life.
(C) The gifts that really most affected my development as a child were books.
(D) I became an avid reader and developed a keen interest in literature and language studies.

keen *(adj)*:
strong; intense

excel *(v)*:
to succeed at; to be good at

stimulating *(adj)*:
interesting; producing energy

indulge *(v)*:
to yield to desires; to do something fun but unproductive or unhealthy

critical faculties *(n phrase)*:
the ability to think analytically

Body:

_____   _____   _____   _____   _____   _____

(A) By developing a broad vocabulary through my writing, I was also able to excel in other academic subjects.
(B) I still find this benefit through reading today, in fact.
(C) I developed excellent language skills by doing a lot of reading and found reading to be creatively stimulating.
(D) I started to write my own stories and poems at a young age as a result.
(E) Furthermore, I found that reading relaxed me and helped me deal with stress more effectively.
(F) Reading books had a very positive influence on my life.

Conclusion:

_____   _____   _____   _____   _____

(A) Consequently, I hope to pass this love of books and reading on to my current students, so that they can gain the same benefits I did.
(B) Clearly, those books I received are part of the reason I am a language teacher today.
(C) Because books continue to stimulate my creativity and calm my nerves, I treasure them as much today as I did in childhood.
(D) Instead of indulging in television or computer games, I developed my imagination and critical faculties.
(E) I developed a passion for reading and writing simply because I received books as gifts from early on.

Look back at the ideas you wrote in the blanks for Step 1. Write your own response to the prompt using one of your own ideas or another idea from Step 1.

Response word count: _____ (Suggested word count = 300)

Skill B Q2 Independent

Practice 2

Step 1

Read the question and think of ideas to list in the blanks.

Having strong social programs in a country often means higher tax rates. In your opinion, is it better to live in a society that invests little money in social programs while keeping tax rates low, or would you prefer to live in a society where you are required to pay high taxes but reap the benefits of strong social programs?

High Taxes, Strong Social Programs

- ensure essential infrastructure (schools, roads, hospitals)
- ensure health care and education
- give security in case of illness, unemployment

_____

_____

Low Taxes, Weak Social Programs

- allow people more disposable income
- encourage responsible behavior
- allow freedom to choose services

_____

_____

Now look at the sample response. Think of the role of each sentence within the essay. Look for any transitions that link the ideas. Underline them. Then, put the sentences in the right order.

Introduction:

_____ _____ _____

(A) For this reason, I would have no qualms paying a higher portion of my income in taxes than I would if there were no social programs.
(B) I would prefer to live in a society that values social welfare over individual wealth.
(C) In short, I believe that it is the responsibility of the state to take care of those who cannot take care of themselves.

Body:

_____ _____ _____ _____ _____

(A) Within such economies, the opportunity of monetary success lies with the individual.
(B) This is an every-man-for-himself attitude that is based on a false premise, that is, that everyone has equal opportunities in a free-market economy.
(C) While it is possible for poor people to achieve great success, it is impossible for all poor people to do so.
(D) Some might argue that in a capitalist society, those who work hard enough can accrue wealth and thus won't have to rely on social welfare.
(E) However, such thinking fails to recognize the social conditions in place that allow the rich to get richer while simultaneously ensuring that the poor stay poor.

Conclusion:

_____ _____ _____ _____

(A) Further, it is not just the poor who benefit, as programs such as universal health care, day care, and social security are very important to the middle and upper middle classes as well.
(B) The success of a capitalist society depends on having a lower, middle, and upper class.
(C) In effect, paying taxes is not like giving money away to poor people, as everyone benefits from social programs.
(D) Therefore, because the middle and upper classes rely on the existence of a lower class for their continued comfort, I believe that it is their responsibility to take care of the poor with social welfare programs.

qualm *(n)*:
a feeling of uneasiness or worry; a reservation

portion *(n)*:
a part

welfare *(n)*:
the benefit and well being of

mentality *(n)*:
a way of thinking; a belief system

premise *(n)*:
a basic, fundamental idea or belief

accrue *(v)*:
to gain and increase

Step 3

Look back at the ideas you wrote in the blanks for Step 1. Write your own response to the prompt arguing for the opposite side to the response given.

Response word count: _____ (Suggested word count = 300)

Skill B Q2 Independent

Practice 3

Step 1

Read the question and think of ideas to list in the blanks.

The twentieth century saw great change. In your opinion, what is one change that should be remembered about the twentieth century? Use specific reasons to explain your choice.

Nuclear Fission: Good Development and Change in 20th Century

- Facilitated end of Second World War
- Fission research/splitting of atom led to other scientific development: Nuclear Power
- Brinkmanship: Threat of world destruction prevents superpowers going to war

_____

_____

Nuclear Fission: Bad Development and Change in 20th Century

- Nuclear bombs cause mass destruction
- Terrorists/rogue states develop weapons of mass destruction
- Nuclear capability causes world debates and power struggles

_____

_____

Now look at the sample response. Think of the role of each sentence within the essay. Look for any transitions that link the ideas. Underline them. Then, put the sentences in the right order.

Introduction:

_____   _____   _____   _____

(A) For example, the use of nuclear fission in atomic weapons produced a meaningful impact on world politics.
(B) Let us investigate these two changes more closely.
(C) One of the greatest changes that occurred during the 20th century was the development of nuclear fission.
(D) In addition, nuclear fission greatly changed the way energy is produced.

Body:

_____   _____   _____   _____   _____   _____   _____

(A) To continue, the use of nuclear fission in reactors has had a great impact for two reasons.
(B) This effect was so severe, in fact, that atomic weapons became a powerful deterrent against the start of further large-scale wars.
(C) Nations were shocked and awed by the vast devastation they caused.
(D) In other words, they have brought about peace.
(E) To begin, atomic weapons were developed and used during World War II.
(F) Second, unlike the burning of wood or fossil fuels, nuclear reactors produce this energy with very little harm to the environment.
(G) First, they can produce a great quantity of electricity for a relatively low cost.

Conclusion:

_____   _____   _____   _____

(A) Thus, the development of nuclear fission forever changed energy production and the politics of war.
(B) Furthermore, the power generated by nuclear reactors makes for a cheaper, cleaner source of energy.
(C) The development of nuclear weapons and nuclear power were clearly very important in the 20th century, bringing about many fundamental changes to society.
(D) This is because nuclear weapons forever changed how war is practiced.

fission (n):
the process of splitting into parts

meaningful (adj):
important

reactor (n):
a building or piece of equipment in which nuclear reactions take place

deterrent (n):
a factor that influences against a given action

awed (adj):
feeling an overwhelming emotion, such as fear

bring about (v phrase):
to make happen; to effect

fundamental (adj):
basic; essential

Look back at the ideas you wrote in the blanks for Step 1. Write your own response to the prompt arguing for the opposite side to the response given.

Response word count: _____ (Suggested word count = 300)

Practice 4

Step 1

Look at the prompt and try to figure out your task.

People usually learn from their elders; however, younger people can also sometimes teach those older than them. Tell about a time when you learned an important lesson from someone younger than you. Use specific details and examples to tell about your experience.

Read the two ideas for possible responses to the prompt. Write one more idea of your own.

1. Children remind us to use our imagination.

2. Children remind us of what's really important in life.

3. _____

Step 2

Read the sample introduction below. Then, in the space on the next page, try to write body paragraphs for 2 of the ideas above. Try to write 3-5 sentences for each body paragraph. Then read the sample conclusion paragraph.

Introduction:

Two years ago, I thought of nothing but work. My only interest was in things that would improve my resumé and my job prospects. One day, I was looking at my resumé and I realized that I needed to add some volunteer work to it. I decided to spend time with a young boy who had lost his parents in a car accident. I thought I would teach this boy, David, many valuable life lessons and give him a head start in the world. In the end, though, it was David who taught me something.

Body 1:

_____

_____

_____

_____

_____

_____

Body 2:

_____

_____

_____

_____

_____

_____

Conclusion:

Soon, my own imagination started running wild. When I got home, I started writing with no concern for structure or style. What's more, I had no intention of trying to have it published! I was having fun, and that was all that mattered. That is the lesson that David taught me. Now, I do things because I enjoy doing them, not because of how it will look on my resumé.

Now read the sample response on page 102. What similarities and differences do you see with the paragraphs you wrote?

Step 3

Write your own response to the prompt in Step 1. First, think of 2 or 3 ideas for body paragraphs. Then, try to write a response using your ideas.

Response word count: _____ (Suggested word count = 300)

Two years ago, I thought of nothing but work. My only interest was in things that would improve my resumé and my job prospects. One day, I was looking at my resumé and I realized that I needed to add some volunteer work to it. I decided to spend time with a young boy who had lost his parents in a car accident. I thought I would teach this boy, David, many valuable life lessons and give him a head start in the world. In the end, though, it was David who taught me something.

The first project David and I undertook together was to write a story. I thought I would teach him about grammar and how to structure a story the way my high school creative writing teacher had taught me. I imagined that David would grow up to be a great writer and dedicate his first book to me. When we began to write, I was amazed at how fast David came up with ideas. When I tried to slow him down to explain the finer points of composition, he wasn't interested. He had a story to tell, and he didn't care about structure and style. I decided to let him have free reign over the story, and I kept my mouth shut. In the end, it was the best story I'd ever read.

Soon, my own imagination started running wild. When I got home, I started writing with no concern for structure or style. What's more, I had no intention of trying to have it published! I was having fun, and that was all that mattered. That is the lesson that David taught me. Now, I do things because I enjoy doing them, not because of how it will look on my resumé.

prospect (n):
a potential for improvement

head start (n phrase):
an early start; an advantageous beginning

undertake (v):
to do something that involves a lengthy process

structure (v):
to organize

dedicate (v):
to write a letter or page honoring someone

come up with (v phrase):
to make; to create

free reign (n phrase):
unrestricted permission; the permission to do whatever one wants

run wild (v phrase):
to move or operate in an energetic, uncontrolled fashion

Skill B Independent

Practice 5

Step 1

Look at the prompt and try to figure out your task.

It is sometimes said that borrowing money from a friend can harm or damage the friendship. Has borrowing or lending money to a friend ever damaged one of your friendships? Use specific details and examples to explain your answer.

Now look at the outline of a possible response to this prompt. Fill in the blank for responding to this prompt.

Main Idea: Borrowing money can be dangerous to a friendship, but it is, in fact, possible under carefully controlled circumstances.

Details: Three dangers to guard against are resentment, superiority, and inability/failure to repay.

Conclusion: While it is probably best to avoid borrowing money in a friendship,

_____ .

Step 2

Read a sample body paragraph for an essay answering this prompt.

Body:

The first danger is feelings of resentment and/or superiority. A friendship is usually based on equality. As soon as one friend lends the other money, that equality is in jeopardy. The lender is in danger of feeling superior to the borrower and letting these feelings affect his or her behavior and the dynamic of the relationship. On the other hand, the borrower is in danger of resenting the lender for his or her financial position. This resentment can be just as detrimental to the friendship as the feelings of superiority.

Write a thesis statement to match this body paragraph.

_____

_____

Now write an introduction and a conclusion for the prompt in Step 1. Use your thesis statement from Step 2. Try to write 3-5 sentences for each paragraph.

Introduction:

_____

_____

_____

_____

_____

Conclusion:

_____

_____

_____

_____

_____

Now read the sample response on page 106. What similarities and differences do you see with the paragraphs you wrote?

Write your own response to the prompt. First, make a short outline like the example above. Then, try to write a response using your outline.

Response word count: _____ (Suggested word count = 300)

It is often said that a sure way to ruin a friendship is for one friend to lend money to another. While this aphorism may hold some truth, it is by no means unavoidably true. Most people probably know two friends from their lives who serve as a counter-example to this rule. The most useful discourse on the subject would be to identify the possible dangers involved in lending money to friends and discuss how to avoid them.

The first danger is feelings of resentment and/or superiority. A friendship is usually based on equality. As soon as one friend lends the other money, that equality is in jeopardy. The lender is in danger of feeling superior to the borrower and letting these feelings affect his or her behavior and the dynamic of the relationship. On the other hand, the borrower is in danger of resenting the lender for his or her financial position. This resentment can be just as detrimental to the friendship as the feelings of superiority.

A more tangible danger, of course, is inability, or worse, unwillingness, to repay. If the borrower has no clear means or no ultimate desire to get the money back to the lender, then the loan is more likely to function as a gift. In this case, the lender probably had not anticipated this eventuality and will be displeased, feeling that he or she has been taken advantage of.

In all, the dangers can be daunting, and certainly no one should loan or borrow a significant amount of money to and from a friend without careful consideration of the risks. However, under the right circumstances, when there is little risk of feelings of resentment or superiority and when the borrower appears to have the means and will for remuneration, there is no reason to rule out such pecuniary arrangements between friends.

aphorism *(n)*:
a brief statement of truth; an adage

discourse *(n)*:
a verbal exchange; a logical conversation

resentment *(n)*:
a feeling of anger or indignation

in jeopardy *(adj phrase)*:
in danger; vulnerable

dynamic *(n)*:
an interactive system or process; the workings and structure of a relationship

detrimental *(adj)*:
harmful

tangible *(adj)*:
noticeable; significant

anticipate *(v)*:
to predict and prepare for

daunting *(adj)*:
very challenging; fearsome

remuneration *(n)*:
the act of paying back a debt

pecuniary *(adj)*:
related to money and payment

Skill B Q2 Opinion

Practice 6

Step 1

Look at the prompt and try to figure out your task.

Do you agree or disagree with the following statement? Only people who earn a lot of money are successful. Use specific reasons and examples to support your answer.

Now look at the outline of a possible response to this prompt. Write one more idea of your own.

1. Society uses other factors to measure success, such as prestige, family, and position in the community.

2. For some professions, such as artist, writer, or actor, just making a living is considered success.

3. _____

Step 2

Read the sample introduction below. Then, in the space on the next page, try to write body paragraphs for 2 of the ideas above. Try to write 3-5 sentences for each body paragraph. Then read the sample conclusion paragraph.

Introduction:

Money is typically considered the measure of success, but is it fair to say that it is the only true measure? Sociologically speaking, the perception of success can involve other factors as well, such as prestige, family, and importance within the community. Furthermore, some professions are highly coveted and difficult to enter. For these, just making a living may be viewed as success in and of itself. Finally, it is possible to think of a situation in which wealth does not translate into success.

Body 1:

_____

_____

_____

_____

_____

_____

Body 2:

_____

_____

_____

_____

_____

_____

Conclusion:

Finally, the reverse situation is sometimes true; that is, a wealthy person is not considered a success. Admittedly, this is the exception to the rule, but examples such as a business person or broker arrested for ethics violations provide a counterpoint. Though they may still be quite wealthy, it would be odd to consider them successful. In sum, money is neither necessary nor sufficient for success.

Now read the sample response on page 110. What similarities and differences do you see with the paragraphs you wrote?

Step 3

Write your own response to the prompt in Step 1. First think of 2 or 3 ideas for body paragraphs. Then, try to write a response using your ideas.

Response word count: _____ (Suggested word count = 300)

Money is typically considered the measure of success, but is it fair to say that it is the only true measure? Sociologically speaking, the perception of success can involve other factors as well, such as prestige, family, and importance within the community. Furthermore, some professions are highly coveted and difficult to enter. For these, just making a living may be viewed as success in and of itself. Finally, it is possible to think of a situation in which wealth does not translate into success.

The word "success" may call to mind a Wall Street stockbroker who earns half a million dollars per year, but other exemplars of success include a well-renowned professor, the head of a well-adjusted family, a chief of police, or a school principal. Any of these people may only make as much money as an unsuccessful stockbroker, but prestige, family, and community status all compensate in the perception of their success.

Other professions in fields such as art, acting, music, or writing may also garner success without money. Given the high percentage of failed artists, actors, and writers who have gone into other professions, anyone who succeeds in making a steady living in these professions is considered to be successful. Indeed, getting by and doing what one loves is a kind of success as well.

Finally, the reverse situation is sometimes true; that is, a wealthy person is not considered a success. Admittedly, this is the exception to the rule, but examples such as a business person or broker arrested for ethics violations provide a counterpoint. Though they may still be quite wealthy, it would be odd to consider them successful. In sum, money is neither necessary nor sufficient for success.

perception (n):
a belief; an opinion

prestige (n):
the condition of being highly respected

coveted (adj):
desired; sought after

translate into (v phrase):
to equal; to produce

exemplar (n):
a thing or person that stands as an example

renowned (adj):
famous

compensate (v):
to provide a benefit in exchange for work or suffering

garner (v):
to get; to achieve; to earn

violation (n):
an act against a rule or principle

sufficient (adj):
enough for a given purpose or need

Vocabulary Review

Vocabulary Review 1

Instructions: Choose the best word or phrase to complete each sentence.

1. The scientific achievements of Albert Einstein _____ those of almost every other scientist in history.
   - (A) deem
   - (B) emit
   - (C) astound
   - (D) outshine

2. Alexander the Great's army was able to _____ many nations as it swept across Europe.
   - (A) emit
   - (B) subdue
   - (C) validate
   - (D) ingest

3. The _____ taxes were increased in order to buy more buses for the city.
   - (A) municipal
   - (B) intangible
   - (C) meager
   - (D) specious

4. The money raised from this concert will go to a charity that helps build _____ such as hospitals and schools in developing countries.
   - (A) concessions
   - (B) burdens
   - (C) disdain
   - (D) infrastructure

5. The students are going to _____ an experiment to determine the melting point of cotton.
   - (A) buy into
   - (B) carry out
   - (C) rage on
   - (D) come to mind

6. All plants and animals rely on light _____ from the sun.
   - (A) emitted
   - (B) validated
   - (C) condemned
   - (D) outshined

7. Some scientists treat Native American claims to archaeological remains with _____, rather than honoring such claims.
   - (A) disdain
   - (B) tribute
   - (C) entourage
   - (D) burden

8. Her accusation that I cheated on the exam was _____. There was no truth to it whatsoever.
   - (A) plausible
   - (B) exempt
   - (C) federal
   - (D) unfounded

9. Over one thousand years ago, the _____ of modern-day Mexicans built some of the largest pyramids in the world.
   - (A) stances
   - (B) ancestors
   - (C) carcasses
   - (D) phenomena

10. Murder is one act that is _____ by almost all modern and ancient cultures.
    - (A) deemed
    - (B) bought into
    - (C) condemned
    - (D) revered

11. Genghis Khan is considered by many historians to be a great military _____. His plans helped the Mongols conquer much of Eurasia.

(A) feat
(B) firearm
(C) strategist
(D) deterrent

12. The Roman Empire demanded large _____ from the lands it conquered.

(A) mastiffs
(B) spectacles
(C) concubines
(D) tributes

13. The owners of the stadium are negotiating with the owners of the hockey team over rights to the _____ sold at hockey games.

(A) concessions
(B) hallmarks
(C) infrastructure
(D) entourage

14. They are relying on new investments to bring success and _____ to the company.

(A) dynamic
(B) pseudoscience
(C) prosperity
(D) reproducibility

15. My parents always recommend that I avoid making _____ decisions. They always want me to think things through.

(A) feasible
(B) hasty
(C) top notch
(D) touchy

Instructions: Choose the word or phrase closest in meaning to the underlined part.

16. Graduating from university was the greatest <u>accomplishment</u> of my life.

(A) discourse
(B) feat
(C) disdain
(D) premise

17. It is a <u>deceptively attractive</u> theory. It sounds logical, but it is based on incorrect assumptions.

(A) brutal
(B) hierarchical
(C) intangible
(D) specious

18. They are having a <u>national</u> election tomorrow. The voters will choose a new leader for the country.

(A) meager
(B) municipal
(C) touchy
(D) federal

19. If all the employees work a little overtime, it is <u>feasible</u> that the project be completed by next week's deadline.

(A) meaningful
(B) plausible
(C) keen
(D) undue

20. The annual migration of cranes is an <u>event</u> that occurs each fall in this region.

(A) stance
(B) portion
(C) strategist
(D) phenomenon

21. She was <u>very surprised</u> when she received an A on her paper. She had thought she had done very poorly.

    (A) validated
    (B) ingested
    (C) tarnished
    (D) astounded

22. His theory on the origins of corn farming has recently been <u>proven true</u> by further research.

    (A) bought into
    (B) revered
    (C) validated
    (D) condemned

23. Parents of babies just learning to crawl must be particularly careful to ensure they do not <u>consume</u> poisonous materials.

    (A) ingest
    (B) deem
    (C) subdue
    (D) cast doubt on

24. Many Native American peoples along the Pacific coast <u>greatly respected</u> the killer whale. In fact, they still do today.

    (A) tarnished
    (B) revered
    (C) engaged in
    (D) took place

25. The government is arguing about whether or not to ban all <u>guns</u> in the country.

    (A) prospects
    (B) campaigns
    (C) firearms
    (D) violations

26. Having large crowds of faithful fans is one of the <u>hallmarks</u> of a successful sports franchise.

    (A) ancestors
    (B) tag markers
    (C) burdens
    (D) spectacles

27. Unfounded conspiracy theories suggested by crackpots often garner <u>unnecessary</u> attention, while legitimate work gets ignored.

    (A) exempt
    (B) undue
    (C) intangible
    (D) hierarchical

28. Because of the snow storm, only a <u>very small</u> number of students attended class today.

    (A) feasible
    (B) federal
    (C) top notch
    (D) meager

29. The Spanish used <u>large attack dogs</u> to help conquer nations in the New World.

    (A) phenomena
    (B) burdens
    (C) mastiffs
    (D) concubines

30. She refuses to change her <u>point of view</u> despite all the evidence that it is incorrect.

    (A) qualm
    (B) stance
    (C) carcass
    (D) prosperity

Instructions: Write the missing words. Use the words below to fill in the blanks.

hierarchical	plausible	campaigns	ancestors	strategist
lingua franca	entourage	engaged in	validate	concubine

Though many historians contend that Hernando Cortes was the military **(31)** _____ behind the successful **(32)** _____ in the New World, a strong case can be made that Malintzin was the true conqueror of the Aztec Empire. Reportedly his **(33)** _____, she was definitely part of Hernando Cortes's **(34)** _____ as he made his way across modern-day Mexico. As a speaker of Nahua, the **(35)** _____ of Mexico at that time, it was Malintzin who actually **(36)** _____ negotiations with the powerful leaders of the nations standing between Cortes and the Aztecs. Indeed, because her **(37)** _____ were part of the noble class, she would have been familiar with the customs and **(38)** _____ nature of the culture. Nahua depictions of the couple, with Malintzin shown in the position of power, tend to **(39)** _____ the idea that she was in control. This evidence, in combination with Spanish reports of her importance in the conquest, makes the idea of Malintzin as conqueror a **(40)** _____ theory.

Instructions: Choose the one word that does not belong.

41.	undue	subdue	conquer	capture
42.	carry out	take place	ingest	engage in
43.	deem	tarnish	conclude	consider
44.	belief	condemn	opinion	stance
45.	welfare	campaign	firearm	strategist

Instructions: Label each pair of words as similar (S) or opposite (O).

46. _____ prosperity   wealth

47. _____ hasty   slow

48. _____ disdain   revere

49. _____ astound   surprise

50. _____ feasible   unfounded

Vocabulary Review 2

Instructions: Choose the best word or phrase to complete each sentence.

1. She _____ at all subjects in school because she studies all the time.
   - (A) indulges
   - (B) accrues
   - (C) excels
   - (D) dedicates

2. The company decided to hire him because of his _____. They believed he'd be a useful asset when analyzing market trends.
   - (A) free reign
   - (B) critical faculties
   - (C) lingua franca
   - (D) tag markers

3. I've only completed a small _____ of my homework. I'll have to stay up all night in order to finish it.
   - (A) portion
   - (B) qualm
   - (C) welfare
   - (D) reactor

4. He doesn't have the right _____ to be a police officer. He always believes everything people say.
   - (A) fission
   - (B) prospect
   - (C) aphorism
   - (D) mentality

5. The city is building a nuclear _____ that will provide electricity to all the houses and businesses within 500 km.
   - (A) discourse
   - (B) reactor
   - (C) prestige
   - (D) premise

6. Many people contend that severe punishments act as a _____ against serious crimes.
   - (A) resentment
   - (B) perception
   - (C) dynamic
   - (D) deterrent

7. After completing a three-month training course, she now has many job _____ to choose from.
   - (A) prospects
   - (B) aphorisms
   - (C) remunerations
   - (D) exemplars

8. If we leave home at 6:00 a.m., we can get a _____ on the rush hour traffic.
   - (A) free reign
   - (B) dynamic
   - (C) head start
   - (D) deterrent

9. She _____ her first novel to the memory of her mother, who tragically died before the book was published.
   - (A) anticipated
   - (B) translated
   - (C) compensated
   - (D) dedicated

10. The professor has given us _____ to come up with our own essay topics, but I'm having trouble coming up with an idea without any restrictions.
    - (A) remuneration
    - (B) violation
    - (C) head start
    - (D) free reign

11. The _____ among students continued to grow after the professor inexplicably cancelled a third consecutive class.
    (A) perception
    (B) resentment
    (C) prestige
    (D) aphorism

12. Unless the government enacts laws limiting cars and factories, pollution will continue to have _____ effects on the environment.
    (A) detrimental
    (B) pecuniary
    (C) sufficient
    (D) fundamental

13. If we pay close attention to the clouds and the wind, we can often _____ the next day's weather.
    (A) compensate
    (B) anticipate
    (C) garner
    (D) accrue

14. Granting government contracts to family members is a _____ of rules on ethics.
    (A) perception
    (B) discourse
    (C) violation
    (D) premise

15. I don't have a _____ amount of money to pay for lunch. Could you lend me five dollars?
    (A) sufficient
    (B) renowned
    (C) coveted
    (D) daunting

Instructions: Choose the word or phrase closest in meaning to the underlined part.

16. I can't wait to go to archaeology class! Those lectures are always so <u>interesting</u>. Let's go!
    (A) stimulating
    (B) daunting
    (C) astounding
    (D) condemning

17. She's having some <u>reservations</u> about the trip to Africa. She's worried about being attacked by lions or elephants.
    (A) perceptions
    (B) violations
    (C) qualms
    (D) cramps

18. The <u>basic idea</u> behind that movie was too unbelievable. Therefore, I don't recommend you go see it.
    (A) fission
    (B) fusion
    (C) prestige
    (D) premise

19. Climbing Mount Everest can be a <u>challenging and fearsome</u> prospect.
    (A) renowned
    (B) sufficient
    (C) cataclysmic
    (D) daunting

20. Her new film is <u>earning</u> a lot of praise and attention from movie critics.
    (A) garnering
    (B) anticipating
    (C) undertaking
    (D) structuring

21. My grandfather is always repeating <u>adages</u> that he thinks will give us some wisdom about how to deal with life's problems. Actually, sometimes they are quite helpful.

(A) deterrents
(B) burdens
(C) aphorisms
(D) pseudonyms

22. Working hard and choosing a profession that one enjoys can <u>produce</u> a happy, satisfying life.

(A) run wild
(B) discourse
(C) translate into
(D) deprive

23. Einstein was <u>famous</u> for his work in the field of physics.

(A) detrimental
(B) renowned
(C) fundamental
(D) keen

24. Though widespread, the <u>belief</u> that baseball is the least interesting sport is not shared by the few true fans of the game.

(A) perception
(B) violation
(C) concession
(D) equation

25. Medicine and law are two of the most <u>sought-after</u> career choices among freshmen students.

(A) hierarchical
(B) pecuniary
(C) coveted
(D) collaborative

26. That diet and exercise plan my doctor prescribed has really made a <u>significant</u> difference in my energy level. I no longer fall asleep during my afternoon classes!

(A) tangible
(B) stimulating
(C) plausible
(D) tedious

27. A skilled novelist spends a lot of time and energy in <u>organizing</u> the sequence of actions in the story.

(A) undertaking
(B) dedicating
(C) diverting
(D) structuring

28. Many people argue that the government should spend money on <u>important</u> matters, like curing cancer, instead of on the exploration of space.

(A) meaningful
(B) keen
(C) unfounded
(D) rigorous

29. One of the <u>essential</u> characteristics of the Renaissance was the shift in focus from God to man.

(A) fundamental
(B) sufficient
(C) municipal
(D) initial

30. If you put money into a bank account, it will <u>gain</u> interest over time.

(A) indulge
(B) accrue
(C) excel
(D) deem

Instructions: Write the missing words. Use the words below to fill in the blanks.

discourse	touchy	burden	pecuniary	undertake
dynamic	welfare	tarnish	exempt	remuneration

One phenomenon that can **(31)** _____ or even destroy the **(32)** _____ of a friendship between two people is the entering into a **(33)** _____ relationship; that is, one friend lending money to the other. While it may be admirable for one friend to be concerned about the financial **(34)** _____ of the other, a detailed schedule for **(35)** _____ should be made before any money changes hands. Beforehand, it is wise for the two friends to **(36)** _____ a lengthy, detailed **(37)** _____ on the subject, discussing the dates and amounts to be repaid and any penalties that may occur if this schedule is not met. Many friends believe their relationships to be **(38)** _____ from the stress of lending and borrowing; however, money matters are generally a very **(39)** _____ subject. Outstanding debt between friends can become an undue **(40)** _____ and strain on the friendship. It is best, therefore, to avoid lending or borrowing if at all possible.

Instructions: Write the missing words. Use the words below to fill in the blanks.

in	top	up	on	into

41. We have to come _____ with an idea for our group project.

42. If I don't do well on the final exam, my passing this course will be _____ jeopardy.

43. Don't buy _____ everything a professor says. It's always a good idea to question what you are being taught.

44. The debate over property rights will rage _____ for decades to come.

45. She wants to go to a _____ notch graduate school in order to ensure a prosperous career in medicine.

Instructions: Match the words that are opposites.

46. compensate   (A) scant

47. discourse   (B) steal

48. undertake   (C) deprive

49. keen   (D) silence

50. indulge   (E) avoid

Chapter 3

Focus: Writing Grammar

Focus | Writing Grammar

Tips

When you review your essay, these tips can help you make it better:

- Check for errors in tense.
  Example If the train <u>come</u> on time, I will not be late. (comes)

- Check for word forms.
  Example The government's decision was very <u>disappointed</u>. (disappointing)

- Make certain each verb agrees with its subject.
  Example The <u>abuse</u> of diplomatic and economic sanctions against polluters <u>is</u> unreasonable and extreme.

- Avoid sentence fragments and run-ons.
  Example Fragment: I met Ann. But not John.
  (I met Ann but not John. OR I met Ann, but I didn't meet John.)
  Run-on: She lives in Canada her parents live in France.
  (She lives in Canada. Her parents live in France.)

- Make sure sentences are connected using the appropriate conjunctions or adverbs.
  Example Andrea wants to eat pizza, <u>so</u> Casey wants to eat chicken. (but/however)

Focus A - Word Forms and Uses

Verb forms and tenses

When you review your essay, consider common mistakes with verbs.

- The verb should agree with its subject.

    Example   Watching certain television programs are a good way to educate children. (X)

    The man waiting for the campers were the park ranger. (X)

- *Be* verbs are used as helping verbs only in the passive voice and the continuous tense.

    Example   Issues related to global warming are not easily resolved. (passive)

    They have been examining the damage of the hurricane. (continuous)

    He was met a very famous poet. (X)

- Auxiliaries and modals should reflect the correct tense/voice of the sentence.

    Example   They had already fallen asleep when I came back. (past perfect)

    If she finds the answer, she will be really happy. (conditional)

    The teacher suggested that he do some research. (subjunctive)

- The summary of a lecture or reading should be written in the present tense.

    Example   The professor argues that fossil fuels are relatively cheap.

    The professor argued that fossil fuels are relatively cheap. (X)

- The same modal verbs can have their own past forms and "have (has) + past participle" depending on how they are used.

    Example   We must admit it. We had to admit it.

    It can't be the solution. It can't have been the solution.

Exercise 1

Find the eight (8) errors in tense in each of the paragraphs below. Correct the errors. There can be more than one incorrect word within a sentence.

1. The reading introduces the idea of supply and demand. In particular, the passage explain that a person's salary depended on public demand for his or her talent. In other words, a person with a rare talent should earns more according to this model because supply was limited while demand is high. The professor gives several specific examples of this theory in action. First, she talks about ordinary people who was made small salaries, such as bus drivers and fast-food workers. Then, she talked about people with special skills, and she point out that they earn significantly more per hour because of their skills. As extreme examples, the professor talks about movie stars and athletes. These people earned thousands or even hundreds of thousands of dollars per hour based on public demand for their rare talents.

2. I know a lot of people who treats their pets as family members. In fact, one of my
have a cat since she was in elementary school. The cat was rather old now, but my friend takes good
care of her. Actually, I think my friend spent too much time and money on her cat. Sometimes, I feel
that she neglects her friends because she has to something for her cat, such as feed it or taken it to
the veterinarian. In my opinion, it is unhealthy for people to focus so much attention on animals. If they
focused this same energy and attention on people around them, it would to make a world of difference.
They could spends the money wasted on pet food and toys on more useful pursuits like treating their
friends or donating to charities!

Exercise 2

Write the correct form of the verb.

A. The reading passage **(1)** _____ (describe) important space achievements in the 20th century,
including NASA's lunar missions. In the lecture, the professor emphasizes the point that US astronauts
are the only humans who have **(2)** _____ (walk) on the moon. He gives several interesting
statistics related to lunar programs **(3)** _____ (develop) by other countries. In particular, the
professor **(4)** _____ (discuss) Russia's lunar program. He points out that although Russia has
sent rockets to the moon, no Russian cosmonauts **(5)** _____ (be) ever sent to land on the
moon. He also mentions that China is **(6)** _____ (develop) plans to send humans to the moon,
though those plans will not materialize for a long time.

B. In order to stay healthy, I walk whenever I can. This often means that I have to **(1)** _____
(plan) my day carefully so that I can leave enough time to get where I need to go. For example,
if I **(2)** _____ (take) the subway to my university, it takes about thirty minutes to get from
my apartment to my classroom. However, if I get off the subway one stop early in order to walk
for exercise, it **(3)** _____ (take) forty-five minutes to get to my classroom. Therefore,
I **(4)** _____ (have) to leave my apartment fifteen minutes earlier than normal so that I can
exercise for fifteen minutes by walking to class. By walking to class, I can also enjoy the added
benefit of relaxing in the fresh air rather than being **(5)** _____ (cramp) and **(6)** _____
(push) around on the crowded subway.

Word Forms and Uses

It is helpful to know word endings in order to use the correct word form. Some words have the same form for different parts of speech.

Noun	-acy, -nce, -ness, -ism, -ion, -ity, -ment, -ure, -al
Adjective	-able, -al, -ant, -ful, -ic, -ish, -ive, -less, -ing, -ed
Verb	-ate, -en, -ify, -ize

Same Form

practice (v=n), appeal (v=n), comment (v=n), cause (v=n), complete (v=adj), individual (n=adj), potential (n=adj)

Other examples

division / divisive / divide	affection / affected / affect	retirement / retiring / retire
validity / valid / validate	exposure / exposed / expose	offense / offensive / offend
failure / failed / fail	threat / threatening / threaten	benefit / beneficial / benefit
efficiency / efficient	disposal / disposable / dispose	responsibility / responsible

It is also helpful to know the position in which each part of speech can be used. Nouns cannot be used in the position of verbs. Adjectives are placed before the nouns that they modify or after a linking verb such as *be*, *become*, or *seem*.

Exercise 3

Choose the correct form of the word.

1. The group leader made an excellent _____ for the new project.
    (A) suggest   (B) suggestion   (C) suggestive

2. Although the temperature was quite high, the _____ was almost zero.
    (A) humidity   (B) humidify   (C) humid

3. The group's _____ ensured that they won in the end.
    (A) competitiveness   (B) competitive   (C) compete

4. No one knew who was _____ for the accident.
    (A) responsibility   (B) responsible   (C) responsibly

5. It was obviously a difficult situation, but he remained _____.

    (A) optimism   (B) optimize   (C) optimistic

6. The company's _____ to plan for changes in the market led to its bankruptcy.

    (A) failure   (B) failed   (C) fail

7. The newcomer was greeted with genuine _____.

    (A) affection   (B) affective   (C) affected

8. Try to find a number that can _____ both numeral A and numeral B.

    (A) division   (B) divide   (C) divisive

9. Many people in the audience found his jokes _____.

    (A) offense   (B) offended   (C) offensive

10. Over the past few decades, the age of _____ has actually risen.

    (A) retirement   (B) retire   (C) retired

11. Researchers in the US and Europe have yet to _____ the findings reported by the Australian company.

    (A) validation   (B) validate   (C) valid

12. Until an environmentally safe method for the _____ of nuclear waste can be found, construction of new reactors will continue to inspire debate.

    (A) disposal   (B) disposes   (C) disposable

13. Whenever skin is _____ to direct sunlight, there is chance of damage to the skin.

    (A) exposure   (B) exposed   (C) exposable

14. Most people find the weather on the island more than _____; they find it pleasant.

    (A) tolerance   (B) tolerate   (C) tolerable

15. Voters felt that she was not _____ enough during her term as governor.

    (A) decisive   (B) decision   (C) decide

16. There are clear pros and cons related to the debate over whether or not to _____ drugs.

    (A) legality   (B) legalize   (C) legal

Find the five (5) incorrect words in each of the paragraphs below. Correct the words. There can be more than one incorrect word within a sentence.

Both the reading and the lecture focus on the connect between poverty and single-parent families, in particularity, families headed by women. The reading describes a government study that looked at all families headed by women across the US. This study concluded that the number of families headed by women below the poverty line decreased from 1960 until the present. The lecture discusses a similarity study that found very different results. In the lecture, the professor says that researchers looked at only poor families headed by women. Between 1960 and the present, the number of poor families headed by women rose from 25 percent to over 50 percent. Thus, the professor correlation poverty to gender of household heads. In her words, the "feminization of poverty" is a real in modern society.

It is often said that the child years are the most important years of one's life. However, I think a person's young adulthood years are more important than the childhood years. As a child, a person spends time either in school or simply playing with friends. School may teach the child information or even certain skills necessity for life, but I think these are generic experiences for just about everyone. When a person becomes a young adult, on the other hand, he or she can truly individual himself or herself. In university, one has the opportune to make decisions without direction from parents or teachers. Of course, the actions each person decides to take can have a significance impact on the course of the rest of his or her life, unlike decisions typically open to children.

Focus B - Sentence Formation

Combining Sentences with Adjective Clauses

An adjective clause modifies a noun or pronoun. Adjective clauses are led by relative pronouns such as *who*, *which*, and *that*. For a noun of time or place, *when* or *where* can be used instead of the phrase *at which*.

When using adjective clauses, consider these common mistakes.

- When the subject noun is modified by an adjective clause, make sure the main verb of the independent clause agrees with the subject that comes before the adjective clause.

  Example   A *person* who works part-time usually <u>receives</u> no benefits.
  People who work part-time usually <u>receive</u> no benefits.

- Use commas before and after an adjective clause if the noun it describes is a specific person or thing, for example, a proper noun.

  Example   Rachel Kingsley, who writes mystery novels, is signing books at the bookstore.
  The writer who is signing books at the bookstore is Rachel Kingsley.

- If the noun is general, you may substitute *that* for *who* and *which*. Don't use commas if the adjective clause begins with *that*.

  Example   The ticket that I needed in order to get onto the plane was not in the packet.
  The ticket, that I needed in order to get onto the plane, was not in the packet. (X)

- If the relative pronoun follows a preposition, the preposition can be in two positions: 1) before the relative pronoun or 2) at the end of the adjective clause.

  Example   The speed <u>at which</u> the wheel turns is measured in revolutions per second.
  The speed <u>that</u> the wheel turns <u>at</u> is measured in revolutions per second.

- *Which* can refer to the whole previous sentence.

  Example   He tried to apologize, which made her even angrier.

- Participle phrases can be formed by reducing adjective clauses.

  Example   Adjective clauses → The audience, <u>which was</u> listening intently to the music, failed to notice the commotion that grew louder and louder in the theater's lobby.
  Reduced adjective clauses → The audience, listening intently to the music, failed to notice the commotion growing louder and louder in the theater's lobby.

Exercise 1

For each sentence below, underline the incorrect part or parts of the sentence.

1. The designation of an individual's class, which can be based on a number of different factors, have been of key interest to sociologists for decades.

2. A child is only a few weeks old is capable of imitating a limited range of facial expressions that he or she observes from a care-giver.

3. Children who grow up in single-parent households typically do worse in school than children what are from two-parent households.

4. Diana Pearce who was an economist by profession suggested a theory that proved popular among sociologists.

5. The female lion, that is distinguished from the male by the lack of a mane, does the hunting.

6. A critical aspect of learning to read involves the integration of skills when develop at different stages of childhood, namely the ability to decipher sounds of a language and the ability to write.

7. One of the most influential theories related to cognitive development comes from Piaget who based his theory on observations of elementary-age children.

8. Paper products, that are made with at least 60% recycled fibers, consume 45% fewer raw materials than products made without recycled fibers.

9. The professor describes the Industrial Revolution as a time at when great strides were made in science and technology.

10. A utopian society is one in that citizens live in perfect fairness and harmony with each other.

11. Polaris, can be located easily on a clear night, is a reliable point in the sky to navigate by because it is located over the point of true north.

12. The claim that "laughter is the best medicine" are supported by research that shows laughter reduces stress, which contributes to a person's overall health and well-being.

Exercise 2

Combine two simple sentences to make a complex sentence containing an adjective clause. Add commas if necessary. Then put parentheses around the relative pronoun and the verb IF they can be omitted.

1. The bowl was found in the cave. It was over 1,000 years old.

   _____.

2. A child knows he did something wrong. He will not look an adult in the eye.

   _____.

3. Cats were important in ancient Egyptian culture. Egyptian culture flourished in the Nile River Valley for thousands of years.

_____.

4. The desk was broken. It was removed from the classroom.

_____.

5. Columbus grew up in a large port city. This city was located on the coast of Italy.

_____.

6. The fossil was obviously a species of horse. The species is now extinct.

_____.

7. People grow up near the border. They usually learn to speak two languages.

_____.

8. The legal age of adulthood is 21. At the age of adulthood, a person can purchase alcohol.

_____.

9. Snoopy is a famous cartoon dog. Snoopy is a beagle.

_____.

10. Two critics reviewed the book. They did not agree.

_____.

11. The university has recently changed its admission policy. The policy used to prohibit women from studying there.

_____.

12. By definition, sunrise is a time in the morning. At this time, the sun first appears over the horizon.

_____.

Combining Sentences with Different Connectors

When writing sentences that are closely related, the writer must use certain techniques to combine the sentences. Various methods can be used to present the same meaning.

Example I did my best, but it was not good enough. (coordinating conjunction)
I did my best; however, it was not good enough. (coordinating adverb)
Although I did my best, it was not good enough. (subordinating conjunction)
Since arriving, we have visited many places. (participle phrase)

When connecting sentences and ideas, consider these common mistakes.

1. Sentence fragments:
We went home. And watched TV. (no subject)
→ We went home and watched TV.

They were happy with the program. But not the board. (no subject or verb)
→ They were happy with the program, but the board were not.

They agreed. Because it was more urgent. (dependent clause used independently)
→ They agreed because it was more urgent.

2. Run-on sentences:
They are happy with the program it is user friendly. (no connecting word or punctuation mark)
→ They are happy with the program. It is user friendly. OR They are happy with the program because it is user friendly.

Punctuation is also important. Look at the differences in punctuation in these sentences.
I was often late because I had to help her. (subordinating conjunction)
Because I had to help her, I was often late (subordinating conjunction + comma)
I had to help her, so I was often late. (comma + coordinating conjunction)
I had to help her. Therefore, I was often late. (coordinating adverb + comma)
I had to help her; therefore, I was often late. (semicolon + coordinating adverb + comma)
NOTE: I had to help her. So, I was often late. (informal, so best avoided in an essay)

Exercise 3

Indicate whether the sentence is correct (C) or incorrect (IC). Then correct the incorrect sentences.

_____ **1.** Musicians are only able to develop their technical skills through practice therefore they must devote long hours to exercises that develop particular techniques.

_____ **2.** Although Chaco Canyon has been declared a national park, the US government allows Native Americans to continue to live there.

_____ **3.** More and more families must rely on both parents working just to make ends meet because the cost of living continues to rise.

_____ **4.** Confucius did not begin teaching until very late in his life. But had a lasting impact on generations long after his death.

_____ **5.** Fresh fruits and vegetables are delivered to markets early in the morning, so shoppers who want the best quality produce do their shopping when the markets open.

_____ **6.** In 1963, Martin Luther King, Jr. was put in jail for a short time and that same year, his house was bombed.

_____ **7.** Because young children are being exposed to violence and sexually explicit material on television politicians are now debating a new law to censor some shows.

_____ **8.** Companies may directly email customers in order to alert them to special offers. Also, companies are now making use of banner ads on high-traffic Internet websites.

_____ **9.** Most people recall that Narcissus turned into a flower, however few remember what happened to his spurned lover, Echo.

_____ **10.** People can usually recall dreams they have just before they wake up. However, dreams occur throughout the entire night's sleep cycle.

_____ **11.** The researcher studied groups of men from various cultures interestingly he found that men's opinions were very similar across cultures.

_____ **12.** Parents usually don't think twice about letting their children go alone to a mall because they view malls as safe public spaces.

Exercise 4

Combine the sentences in two different ways using the words in parentheses.

1. In the past, you would have to pay for a stamp to send a message to a friend. Today, you can send messages for free using email. (but, whereas)

a. _____

b. _____

2. Many airlines are offering discount tickets for flights. More people are flying for weekend trips to scenic cities. (so, because)

a. _____

b. _____

3. The architect built many famous structures. He established a school of architecture in Arizona. (and, also)

a. _____

b. _____

4. My father did not hold a well-paying job. He enjoyed his job a lot. (although, but)

a. _____

b. _____

5. The epic work follows the lives of forty characters through the revolution. Readers often have trouble keeping track of who is who in the novel. (thus, so)

a. _____

b. _____

6. A driver caught operating a vehicle while intoxicated will be issued a ticket. The owner of the vehicle will receive a ticket as well. (additionally, and)

a. _____

b. _____

Exercise 5

Reduce the adverbial clause into a participle phrase.

Example <u>As they were too young to be left alone</u>, the young birds were taken from the nest and transported to a care facility.

<u>Being too young to be left alone</u>, the young birds were taken from the nest and transported to a care facility.

1. Since the building has been severely damaged by the storm, it has to be torn down.

_____

_____

2. The plastic melted and warped because it had been left in the car on a hot day.

_____

_____

3. We are only able to objectively view the core of the problem after we cut through all of the media hype.

_____

_____

4. Because the town wants to attract more companies, it will offer tax incentives to new businesses.

_____

_____

5. In the past, women were confined to the home by social pressure since they were primarily expected to bear and raise children.

_____

_____

Parallel Structure

In order to make a sentence clear and balanced, it is important to use parallel structures in all parts of the sentence. When words or phrases are connected, those words or phrases should be parallel in terms of their form, tense, and parts of speech. When using conjunctions, make sure the parts of the sentence are balanced or parallel.

- Forms
  I like to jog and lifting weights. (jogging and lifting)

- Tense
  They meet customers and are taking orders. (take)

- Parts of speech
  The plants grew over the walls and some were in the buildings. (over the walls and into the buildings)

Exercise 6

Indicate whether the sentence parts display parallel structure (P) or not (NP). Underline the parts that are or should be parallel.

_____ 1. A student who waits until the last minute to study for an exam and completes assignments in a careless manner will do poorly in the class.

_____ 2. Both by the way the couple dressed and by their interaction with each other, it was obvious they were on their honeymoon.

_____ 3. Job opportunities are increasing in fields related to Internet technology but have decreased in many traditional fields of engineering.

_____ 4. Learning how to write Chinese was harder for me than learning how to speak it.

_____ 5. My father taught me how to drive in reverse and how to parallel park.

_____ 6. Shakespeare wrote comedies, romances, tragedies, and plays based on real people from history.

_____ 7. She spent hours wandering around different floors of the library, enjoying her solitude, and discovering old, interesting books.

_____ 8. Learning to write well is important for business majors because employees at all levels may be required to write reports that are accurate and including important details.

Exercise 7

Underline the phrase that is not parallel to the rest of the sentence. Then change the phrase to make it parallel.

1. A child's voice is higher than an adult.

_____.

2. A family either learns to live within its budget or will risk sinking into debt.

_____.

3. I found most of the books required by the course interesting, informative, and they entertained me.

_____.

4. The violinist played with grace, incredible dexterity, and speed.

_____.

5. A shocking number of freshmen waste their first year of college not studying enough, doing things harmful to their health, and not utilizing the campus facilities available to them.

_____.

6. In the art appreciation course, students will learn to analyze important elements of art and recognizing styles of various art movements.

_____.

7. Most students expect three things out of university: to learn life skills, meeting new friends, and to prepare for their future careers.

_____.

8. The Hopi, the Navajo, and Zuni are three well-known Native American peoples of the southwest United States.

_____.

Read the sample paragraphs. Find four (4) mistakes in each paragraph and correct them.

The reading and the lecture both describe Chomolunga, which are the mountain better known as Mt. Everest. The reading introduces just the basic facts about the mountain, such as its location, height, and how much it snows there. The professor adds to this information by talks about all of the people who have tried to climb Mt. Everest. In particular, he explains that although thousands of people were trying to climb the mountain, only about 650 have succeeded. On top of that, 142 of those successful climbers died before they made it back down the mountain. Obviously, Mt. Everest is an incredible and dangerous mountain.

In my opinion, teamwork is a more valuable asset in a new employee than independence. Most jobs cannot be done alone therefore it is necessary for employees to be able to work both with colleagues what work within the same company as well as with individuals or teams from other companies. Employees must have the necessary skills to communicate effectively with others as well as cooperate in forming strategies or solutions for workplace tasks and problems. Although an independent employee might be able to do certain tasks without help or input from others, these are not the most efficient workers. Because the tasks he or she undertakes are smaller or more limited in nature than the tasks which can undertake by teams.

Practice Test

Practice Test

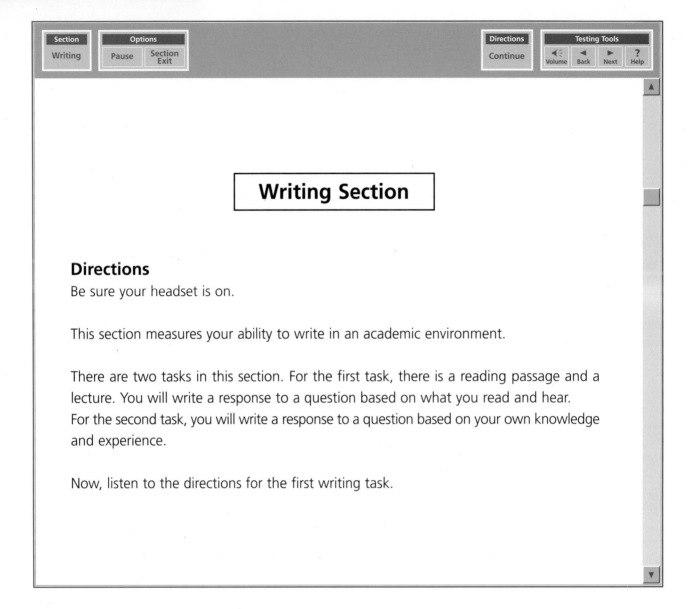

Writing Section

Directions

Be sure your headset is on.

This section measures your ability to write in an academic environment.

There are two tasks in this section. For the first task, there is a reading passage and a lecture. You will write a response to a question based on what you read and hear. For the second task, you will write a response to a question based on your own knowledge and experience.

Now, listen to the directions for the first writing task.

Section
Writing

Options
Pause | Section Exit

Directions
Continue

Testing Tools
Volume | Back | Next | Help

Integrated Writing Directions

For this task, you will have three minutes to read a passage about an academic topic. You may take notes while reading if you wish. The passage will then disappear and you will hear a lecture about the same topic. While listening, you may also take notes.

You will then have 20 minutes to write a response to a question related to the relationship between the lecture and the reading passage. Answer the question as completely as possible using information from both the reading passage and the lecture. The question will not ask you to express a personal opinion. The reading passage will appear again when it is time for you to start writing. You may use your notes from the lecture and the reading to help you answer the question.

Typically, an effective response for this task will be 150 to 225 words long. Your response will be graded on the quality of your writing and on the completeness and accuracy of the information you include in your response. If you finish your response before your time has run out, you may click **Next** to go to the second writing task.

Now, you will see the reading passage for three minutes. Remember that the passage will be available to you again while you are writing. Immediately after the reading time ends, the lecture will begin. Be sure to keep your headset on until the lecture has ended.

Word Count   0   Hide Undo Cut Paste

Sociology is the study of social groups. We can define a social group as "two or more individuals who have developed a common identity relating to some object or activity." We can further define a social group by specifying four preconditions: there must be interaction among the members, the members must be aware that they are in a group, they must share a common cause or interest, and there must be an organizational structure. Some examples of kinds of social groups are family groups, educational groups, work groups, and friendship groups.

The sociologist, Charles Horton Cooley, introduced the idea of primary and secondary groups. A primary group is a group that is small, usually comprised of 15 to 20 members. These members share intimate and personal communication and maintain strong emotional bonds over an extended period of time. A secondary group lacks one or more of these qualities, such as strong emotional ties.

Some classifications are not technically social groups at all. A peer group is composed of individuals of equal status who interact frequently. A reference group is a group that other individuals use as a standard for some concept or activity. An aggregate is a group of people who are simply in the same place, such as everyone sitting on a train.

As a social group increases in size, its nature changes as well. A bureaucracy is a large and powerful social group characterized by formal organization, hierarchies, and distinct rules and guidelines. Of course, all of these smaller and larger groups interact with each other and make up the supergroup, society. By understanding all of the smaller groups, sociologists hope to ultimately gain a clearer understanding of society as a whole.

🎧 Now listen to part of a lecture on the topic you just read about.

You have 20 minutes to plan and write your response. Your response will be judged on the basis of the quality of your writing and on how well your response presents the points in the lecture and their relationship to the reading passage. Typically, an effective response will be 150 to 225 words.

Question: Summarize the points in the lecture you just heard, explaining how the speaker's definition of society differs from the definition presented in the reading.

Sociology is the study of social groups. We can define a social group as "two or more individuals who have developed a common identity relating to some object or activity." We can further define a social group by specifying four preconditions: there must be interaction among the members, the members must be aware that they are in a group, they must share a common cause or interest, and there must be an organizational structure. Some examples of kinds of social groups are family groups, educational groups, work groups, and friendship groups.

The sociologist, Charles Horton Cooley, introduced the idea of primary and secondary groups. A primary group is a group that is small, usually comprised of 15 to 20 members. These members share intimate and personal communication and maintain strong emotional bonds over an extended period of time. A secondary group lacks one or more of these qualities, such as strong emotional ties.

Some classifications are not technically social groups at all. A peer group is composed of individuals of equal status who interact frequently. A reference group is a group that other individuals use as a standard for some concept or activity. An aggregate is a group of people who are simply in the same place, such as everyone sitting on a train.

As a social group increases in size, its nature changes as well. A bureaucracy is a large and powerful social group characterized by formal organization, hierarchies, and distinct rules and guidelines. Of course, all of these smaller and larger groups interact with each other and make up the supergroup, society. By understanding all of the smaller groups, sociologists hope to ultimately gain a clearer understanding of society as a whole.

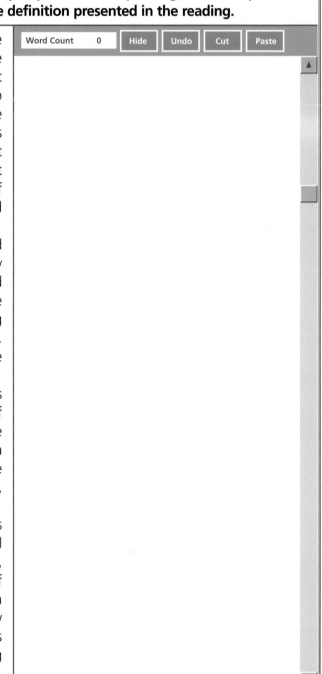

Word Count   0   Hide Undo Cut Paste

Independent Writing Directions

For this task, you will write a response to a question that asks you to present, explain, and support your opinion on an issue. You will have 30 minutes to write your response to the question.

Typically, an effective response for this task will be about 300 words long. Your response will be graded on the quality of your writing. Graders will consider various aspects of the response such as the development of your ideas, the organization of the content, and the quality and accuracy of the language used to express ideas.

If you finish your response before your time has run out, you may click **Next** to end this section.

When you are ready to begin, click on the **Dismiss Directions** icon.

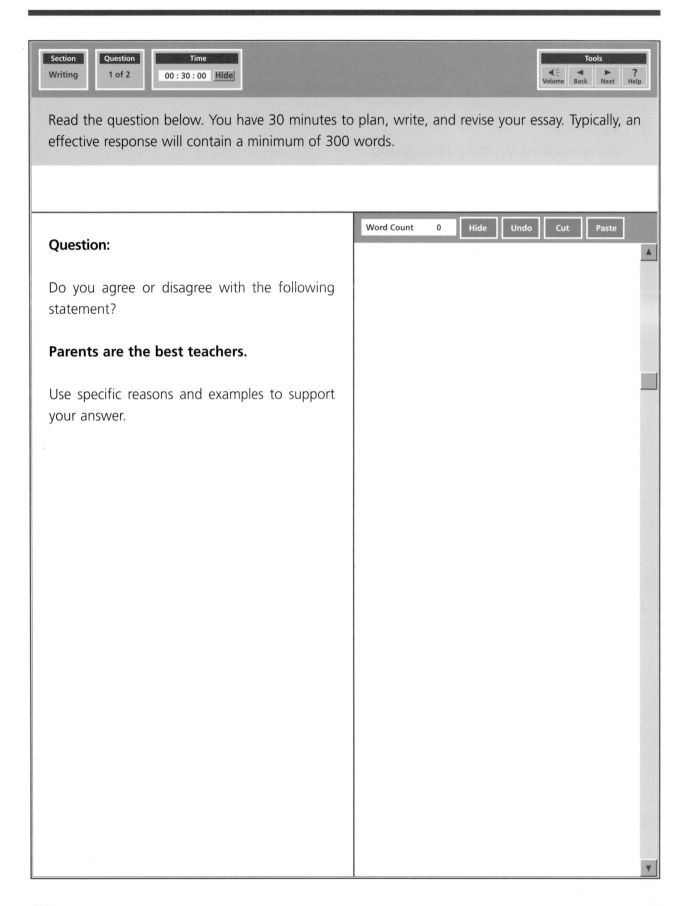

Section
Writing

Question
1 of 2

Time
00 : 30 : 00 Hide

Tools
Volume Back Next Help

Read the question below. You have 30 minutes to plan, write, and revise your essay. Typically, an effective response will contain a minimum of 300 words.

Word Count   0   Hide   Undo   Cut   Paste

Question:

Do you agree or disagree with the following statement?

Parents are the best teachers.

Use specific reasons and examples to support your answer.

Transcripts

Transcripts

Chapter 1

Skill A

Practice 1

01 Statistics

W: I hope you have all read the introduction to Correlation Studies in your textbooks. One component of that reading that I want to stress the importance of is that when assessing the validity of a correlation study it is vital to remember this rule: Correlation does NOT imply causation. It's easy, when you see a correlation, to assume that the changing rate of one variable is causing the changing rate of the other, but how do investigators determine which variable would be the cause and which the effect? Sometimes, it's common sense, but when the investigation itself is not manipulating either variable, it is difficult to know with certainty that one variable is causing the other to occur.

Another danger to be wary of is the possibility of a third variable. Consider this example. Ice cream consumption is positively correlated with drowning. Surprised? What might explain this correlation?

M: Well, maybe the ice-cream could give you a cramp while you're swimming.

W: Okay, maybe. But what if I told you that ice cream consumption is also positively correlated with boating accidents.

M: Okay, well, it's got something to do with the beach, or the water...

W: ...and when do people go to the beach or go boating?

M: In the summer.

W: Exactly — when it's hot. And when do people eat ice cream? When it's hot. The third variable here is the weather. So, just because two events are correlated, it doesn't mean that one event is causing the other. It might give us a hint that that might be the case, but further research has to be done to say conclusively that one event causes the other.

For example, smoking is positively correlated with cancer. This evidence alone does not indicate that smoking causes cancer. However, it was the basis for further research that has demonstrated a causal relationship between smoking and cancer.

So, correlation studies are valuable tools that provide a glimpse into how events are related, and they might indicate causal relationships, but alone they in no way determine that one event causes another.

02 History

M: Our topic today is the issue of historiography, specifically revisionist historiography. In many academic circles, the word "revisionism" has come to be used pejoratively. Why do you suppose that is? Well, the reasons are as follows: Whereas some academics still regard historical revisionism as a term simply referring to a re-examination of the past, many historians now believe that revisionism itself has become tinged with a political bias. They argue that many who call themselves "revisionist historians" are in fact hacks and crackpots posing as academics. Due to their own specific ideological leanings, these "revisionist" writers present poorly researched papers or publish controversial books and articles that negate or deny specific events in history. Such writings can be particularly dangerous when non-experts read them. This is because, without fully understanding the context, these readers are influenced to condone or support a controversial and often completely inaccurate historical perspective.

The best and most recent example of this form of historical revisionism is what has been dubbed, "Holocaust Denial." As most of you are aware, the term "holocaust" has come to refer to the war crimes perpetrated by the Nazi regime in Germany between 1933 and 1945 against, predominantly, the Jewish people. Holocaust deniers are those so-called revisionists who claim either that the holocaust never happened or that statistics surrounding the murders of Jews and other victims of the holocaust have been greatly exaggerated. Holocaust deniers and other revisionists deliberately misrepresent and manipulate historical evidence so as to propagate their political bias or to support an ideological bias. Their writing is usually full of logical fallacies and conspiracy theories and without much supportable documentation or verifiable data.

Such so-called revisionists are not only giving the term "historical revisionism" a bad name; they are coloring the entire field in a negative light through their biased and unscientific approach to the past. However, as long as legitimate students and scholars of history remain aware of this trend and work to combat it, genuine historical research and authentically revisionist enterprises can and should continue.

03 Astronomy

W: In today's astronomy lecture, I wish to discuss the theoretical holes that exist in the Big Bang theory. I also want to discuss alternative views of how the universe might have come into being. You have chosen a very tricky area of science to study, because we are dealing with subject matter that is often difficult to verify.

As most of you'll remember if you've read the assigned chapter, the Big Bang theory argues that our universe was created by an explosion that took place around 13.7 billion years ago. Such prestigious figures as Edwin Hubble, for whom the famous Hubble telescope is named, developed and supported this hypothesis. These scientists believed that our universe originated as a small, hot entity that inflated and expanded, then cooled, and now continues to expand.

I want to examine this theory more closely. What is the major evidence supporting it?

We know the universe had an origin, and we know galaxies are moving away from each other. Thanks to Wilson and Penzias, we've also discovered the existence of radiation in space as well as an abundance of Hydrogen and Helium gases that supports the idea that a big explosion occurred.

But this evidence is far too general and vague to be limited to the Big Bang theory. This empirical data also supports other models for how the universe came into being. It is important to remember that the Big Bang theory has never been proven beyond a reasonable doubt. It simply remains a popular and widely acknowledged hypothesis.

A new idea has recently emerged called the ekpyrotic scenario, that's E-K-P-Y-R-O-T-I-C. This theory argues, for example, that our universe was created when two parallel "membranes" of space matter collided. While this theory shares some elements with the Big Bang theory, it also has many differences. It is also supported by the same empirical data I have mentioned. All we can really do at this point, as scientists, is to keep investigating the subject with care and precision and wait for new technologies to uncover new information.

04 English Literature

M: Who wrote Shakespeare, students? The question sounds almost illogical, doesn't it?

You all want to shout out: "Duh, well, Shakespeare did of course. Who else could have written Shakespeare?" If only it were that simple. I'm afraid that in literary studies, things are never quite that simple. That is a good lesson for all of you to learn. Consequently, before we start our analysis of the *Hamlet* text you have so diligently brought along with you to class today, we are going to examine the authorship debate.

There are some literary scholars out there who believe an aristocrat called Edward De Vere actually wrote the plays we think of as Shakespeare's, under a pseudonym. The problem is that the arguments to support this claim are actually rather sketchy and poorly researched. Their notion is, in my opinion, a conspiracy theory with little genuine supportable evidence.

For example, it's true that not one single document categorically states that William Shakespeare of Stratford wrote *King Lear* or *Hamlet*, but then no such document exists for any other playwright of the time either. While the so-called "Antistratfordians" find it mysterious that Shakespeare's signature doesn't appear on the early quartos of his plays and that, in fact, no name appears on them at all, this is actually easy to explain. It is because at that time, contemporary plays weren't considered to be literature. Authorship was not considered particularly relevant or important since theater was considered to be popular art, not serious art. It was only after Shakespeare's death that his colleagues decided to collect his plays and publish them in the so-called "First Folio," in 1623.

There are also numerous extant documents referring to William Shakespeare as actor and playwright. These are easily accessible to the serious scholar. Why would Shakespeare's contemporaries, like playwright Ben Jonson, have referred to him so often by name had it really been a pseudonym? An entire group of artists wouldn't all agree to shield someone's identity without motivation. What could they gain from it? What would the purpose of such a deception have been?

Skill B

Practice 1

M: Psychologists are starting to acknowledge sleep deprivation as a vital factor in children's school performance. They tell us that just one or two more hours of sleep each night can make a substantial improvement in kids' grades. All parents have to do is make their children go to bed earlier. Hmm... Easier said than done, don't you think?

Well, as you read in the textbook, sleep no doubt plays an important role in how well a child performs at school. However, we need to remember that sleep is only one variable in the equation. Indeed, an educator would be remiss in merely prescribing more sleep for all students suffering from low grades. Besides being well rested, children need to be well nourished, too. It's tough to concentrate on an empty stomach. They also need to be well clothed, and, most important of all, they need a stable, loving home life.

If a child struggles at school, it may well be true that he or she did not get the recommended nine hours of sleep the previous night. The question we need to ask ourselves is, "Is that the only factor involved?" What about breakfast? Did the child have pancakes, eggs, toast, and orange juice . . . or just a piece of toast and a glass of water? Did he or she wear a warm coat? Were there holes in his or her shoes? If students have trouble with attention span, could it be because they're still thinking about the knock-down, drag-out fight between Mom and Dad last night? Furthermore, if they have an accident on the playground, were they too tired, too excited, or did they merely slip? What's the impact of lack of sleep vis-à-vis other factors?

The human psyche, especially in children, is fragile, complex, and mysterious. Sleeplessness is a valid concern. However, researchers must consider other variables before jumping to the conclusion that sleep deprivation is the primary cause of academic woes.

Practice 2

M: Today, we'll be talking about non-violent forms of protest. Can anyone give some other terms for this type of action?

W: I think the textbook called it "civil disobedience."

M: Ah, "civil disobedience" very good. Another form is passive resistance. So, you've read that some don't believe civil disobedience to be an effective means of protest, but others, of course, are more supportive.

Let's begin with civil disobedience. You saw that Henry David Thoreau pioneered the modern US theory on this form of non-violence. According to Thoreau, there is no need to physically fight the government as long as you and the government don't support each other in any way. Independence in mind and action is the guiding principle for achieving what is just. In this manner, Thoreau prescribes protesting through justice, rather than physical violence. Civil disobedience derives its power and value because it is "right." This is almost always the principle of peaceful demonstrations in the US today. People, or even nations, can use the principles of civil disobedience to protest companies or nations that they feel are involved in unethical behavior. Rather than using violence, they can boycott, or stop buying, products from that company or country, thus using economics rather than violence to effect change.

Passive resistance is the other form of non-violence we're looking at. Who's the main figure here?

W: Gandhi, right?

M: Good, Gandhi is the non-violent figure par excellence, isn't he? His method involved purposely breaking the law with the expectation of attack by the authorities and then quietly resisting without retaliation. In essence, he attempted to become a martyr. An example is his breaking of the salt tax. Gandhi's followers formed a peaceful blockade around the salt mines and allowed themselves, without resistance, to be brutally beaten by British soldiers. When people around the world, including Britain, got wind of this brutal behavior, they put pressure on the British government to change their ways. Thus, passive resistance was more debilitating than violence to the British colonial infrastructure. Without resorting to violence, Gandhi effectively persuaded the English to end colonial rule in India.

Practice 3

M: Have any of you heard of the term "carbon chauvinism"? Yes, this is science class, and chauvinism has found its way into science. The term, in fact, seeks to discredit views that all life forms are carbon based. But isn't the main question really whether science is being chauvinistic? The answer we'll discuss today is "probably not." In fact, all current scientific evidence indicates that carbon is necessary to life as we know it.

As you all have hopefully read, silicon-based life is one of the pre-eminent contenders to carbon. Yes, the Earth is silicon rich and carbon poor. Yes, tiny diatoms have silicate-based skeletons, but, do we actually have pure silicon life forms to study? We certainly do not. All terrestrial life is carbon based. Rare carbon, rather than the relatively abundant silicon, has proven to be the successful life base on Earth. What about non-terrestrial silicon life? Silicon bonds resist extreme heat better than carbon. This could provide it with the molecular stability for biological evolution on planets closer to the sun. However, the reality is we can't replicate and test such alien environments. Scientifically, we just can't say with certainty.

The other commonly speculated alternative biochemistry base is sulfur. Sulfur is similar to carbon because it's soluble in water. This is an important characteristic on Earth, where water is the medium for all biochemical life. We have, in fact, found some types of bacteria that use sulfur in their metabolism, but these bacteria are still carbon-based life forms, with sulfur playing a secondary metabolic role. Sulfur can form the long molecular chains required for biological evolution, but its high reactivity makes it too unstable to sustain complex, biological evolution here on Earth. We have no pure sulfur life forms on Earth to study! The point is that under conditions for life as we know it, we have no knowledge indicating this is possible.

The key point today is that all conditions for biological life "as we know it" include carbon in their chemistry. We have no empirical data about successful non-carbon biochemistries. So, I'd say the present state of science can't be held guilty of "carbon chauvinism." Alien environments or odd physical conditions are, for the most part, variables we either cannot study or for which there is no real data.

Practice 4

W: How many of you agree with Native American legal rights to archaeological remains? Think of such examples as the Kennewick Man! Wow!... I see the article you read raised some sympathy. Well, I also think scientific communities are taking a hard line with respect to Native American views. In fact, today we'll discuss this subject. Respecting Native American rights to archaeological remains doesn't necessarily mean stopping the progress of science. The problem is that many scientists argue Native American claims spell the end of all research. This is the case with the Kennewick Man, but are Native American claims really so threatening to science? I doubt it. As a matter of fact, I have here a comment from the Union of Confederate Tribes that suggests they are not! "We're not anti-science," they remark. "We just want a say in what happens to our ancestors." To accommodate scientific interests while respecting the dignity and importance of Native American beliefs — shouldn't that be the real goal? Well . . . many Native American groups already show their support of research on archaeological finds, if they are at least consulted or involved! Would you be surprised if I told you that at least 57 Native American groups currently work with scholars on joint archaeological programs? For sure, collaborative work between scientists and Native American leaders is important. It shows the possibility for scientific progress to not only respect Native American communities, but also enlist their participation. Scientists involved in these programs report a lot of advantages to conducting research with the participation of Native Americans. They say deeper understanding of these cultures is obtained by collaborative work. That's right, it enhances their knowledge and can even clarify their scientific results.

It is untrue to say that scientific study would not be possible if Native American beliefs were honored. Attempts to freely pursue science at the cost of Native American beliefs are really the root of the debate. What the Kennewick Man conflict shows is more collaborative work is needed, not efforts to pursue science at all costs.

Chapter 2

Skill A

Practice 1

W: We all know that Hernando Cortes conquered Motecuhzoma and the Aztec empire in the early 16th century, but a lesser known part of the conquest is the story of the secret behind Cortes's success. We know that he landed in Tabasco in 1519 and subdued the smaller nations there. According to the tales, the people of those nations told him of the Aztecs further inland, and he negotiated their support in the conquest. But how was this possible? How do you negotiate with a people whose language you have never heard?

The Spaniards had never set foot in that part of Mexico and had no prior contact with any of its peoples. Cortes did have a priest, Gerónimo, who could speak Yucatec Mayan, a language spoken far to the south. Coincidentally, they encountered a local woman who was bilingual in Mayan and Nahua, the language of the Aztecs, which also happened to be the lingua franca of central Mexico at that time. It was through Gerónimo and this woman, who the Spaniards called, Doña Marina, or Malinche, and who the Mexicans called Malintzin, that Cortes was able to communicate and negotiate with the various peoples he encountered. Cortes took Malintzin into his entourage as his interpreter-slash-concubine. Now, from this point on, his success strategy is clear. Via Malintzin, he wins the support of the many non-Aztec nations and makes his way toward Tenochtitlan, the Aztec capital. It would be difficult for modern historians to know who the real genius was behind the negotiations. Cortes presumably knew very little of local politics, history, and customs, and never communicated directly with any Mexicans, while on the other hand, Malintzin had knowledge of all these things. On top of this is the fact that she was the one who was actually speaking directly to the national leaders. The extent to which she was just repeating interpreted versions of Cortes's Spanish, or whether she was paraphrasing or speaking her own mind, will likely never be known.

By the time Cortes had reached Tenochtitlan, evidence suggests that Malintzin had begun to interpret directly between Spanish and Nahua without using the priest and the unrelated Mayan language as a go-between. Malintzin largely disappears from history after the fall of Tenochtitlan in 1521. We know she bore Cortes a son, who would later gain a high rank before being executed, and that she served as an interpreter again during Cortes's campaign in Honduras.

Some Spanish sources also indicate that she was much more than an interpreter. The soldier Díaz Castillo calls her a "great lady" who was indispensable to the expedition. Another conquistador quotes Cortes as saying that after God, Marina was the main source of his success. Nahua sources typically depict Cortes and Malintzin together, or even her alone as an authority in her own right.

Some sources also indicate that the Aztec would refer to Cortes as "Malintzin" as well, casting further doubt on the hierarchical nature of their relationship. So, the question that arises is "Was Malintzin the true conqueror of the Aztec empire and Cortes and his army merely the means she chose to do so?"

Practice 2

M: Most of you know that there is a new mega-dome being built in our city for our new football team, but did you know that you are helping pay for it? That's right. The federal government allows cities to sell tax-exempt bonds to produce capital to fund stadium construction. This means, on average, that about 70 million dollars in taxes are lost for a 225-million-dollar stadium. That's 70 million of your tax dollars being spent not on education or infrastructure, but on a sports team that makes millions a year in profit anyway.

Some will say that this 70 million dollars is an investment, from which we see returns in the form of local jobs, increased property value, a boost to the local economy, and national publicity for the city. On the surface, this appears to be true, but let's take a closer look at each of these points, one by one.

Does a stadium and sports team create jobs? Well, obviously. A better question is "What kind of jobs does it create?" Well, we have construction jobs to build the stadium and staffing jobs to run it. The construction workers would be employed elsewhere if not for the stadium, most likely at building something that serves a clearer public function, like roads, schools, residences, or business facilities. So, there's no gain here. The low level stadium workers are mostly part-time employees who earn meager wages. What about the players, coaches, and team managers? Well, they no doubt end up with most of the money, but most of these have little involvement in or attachment to the local community, and that money is typically invested elsewhere; or, as you might say, "sucked out of the community."

OK, then. What about all the visiting fans and tax revenue? Well, in theory that sounds nice, but if we look at the numbers...for instance, Baltimore's baseball stadium brings in the most outside fans, thanks to nearby D.C., which didn't have its own team until quite recently. Their annual revenue from that is about 3 million dollars per year. Sounds like a lot, but that's actually quite low for a 200-million-dollar investment. Also, most tax revenue from the stadium is not additional revenue; rather, it replaces tax revenue that would have gone through movie theaters, restaurants, and so on.

Finally, we have the idea that a sports team boosts a city's image, attracting businesses, and so on. Well, first off, this is not really feasible to measure. Also, we have to ask ourselves "Could that 70 million dollars be better spent on other projects that might do more to boost the city's image?" Like what? Well, like top-notch research facilities for the university. Like education and wi-fi infrastructure to attract businesses and families, or even in PR projects for the city. I mean, why not spend 10 million on PR and marketing for the city, rather than 70 million on a sports team that is a profit-seeking business?

Practice 3

W: When scientists in Utah announced they had discovered a way to create cheap energy with little waste, the media grabbed hold of the story. It seemed too good to be true. However, the claim was met with much disdain in the scientific community. The scientists claimed that in their experiment, they observed the creation of an amount of energy too great to be explained by chemical reaction. To explain this finding, they guessed that nuclear fusion was taking place and called it "cold fusion," as it was taking place at room temperature.

The scientific community was astounded and didn't readily buy into the "cold fusion" claim. For one thing, it didn't fit with current theory. Nuclear physicists will tell you that when nuclear fusion takes place, there are protons or neutrons emitted. According to theory, the researchers should have been killed when they did the experiment. However, they weren't. Further, they were unable to detect any extra neutrons or protons. If nuclear fusion necessarily involves the emission of protons and neutrons, and in this experiment they didn't see any excess protons and neutrons, then it couldn't possibly be nuclear fusion . . . unless, of course, the theory is incorrect. You cannot simply dismiss observations because they don't fit with a theory. That's how science works, isn't it? Theories are not facts. When evidence appears to contradict the theory, the theory needs to be reassessed. We cannot throw out observations because they don't fit with current theories. Science would not have progressed very far if we did. We'd still be wandering around thinking the sun and the planets revolved around the Earth!

The scientific method demands that findings need to be replicated in order to validate them. After all, human error can lead to some flawed findings. So, when the "cold fusion" scientists made their announcement, many scientists followed suit and tried to replicate their experiment. They failed. They could not, with measured predictability, reproduce the findings of the original scientists. Following this, the whole idea was dismissed. Some accused the scientists of fraud, while others maintained that there must have been errors in their measurements. Indeed, the equipment used to take the measurements was not very accurate. So, the whole idea of "cold fusion" was deemed by some to be a pseudoscience. It did not stand up to the scientific process.

There's a problem with this stance, though. The scientific process needs time. Just because results weren't replicated in the months following the initial experiment doesn't mean the findings are invalid. Fortunately, some have continued to pursue the idea, and many have, indeed, reproduced the original findings. The equipment used for taking measurements has improved greatly in this time, and is more reliable. While some continue to insist that any positive finding must be erroneous, (and indeed, some findings are erroneous,) no skeptic has been able to identify an error that could explain all of the positive results obtained.

Practice 4

M: The debate about whether or not cannibalism took place in Anasazi society is a touchy subject. The Anasazi are the ancestors of the Pueblo peoples, a collective name for various Native American groups in present-day New Mexico and Arizona. When we look at the more recent history of the Pueblo peoples, we revere them for their peaceful ways and their respectful relationship with the Earth. When evidence suggested that cannibalism took place between 900 and 1300 A.D. in these societies, people were naturally horrified and offended. How could such a peaceful and cooperative group of people have done such a thing? Well, the evidence is sound, and it effectively proves that cannibalism took place, but that does not mean that it was a culturally accepted practice. In fact, one of the leading researchers suggests that it was a method used by foreigners to terrorize the Anasazi.

Let's discuss the evidence. First of all, using basic tag markers of cannibalism, archaeologists have shown that certain skeletal remains of humans were indeed treated like the carcass of an animal. The bones were broken. They also showed signs of having been burned, and indentations from sharp instruments indicate that flesh was intentionally removed. Now, some say that this does not prove that the flesh was eaten and point to a witch slaughter to explain it. However, fossilized fecal matter from the same area shows that human flesh had indeed been digested. Again, this only proves that it happened once, and it doesn't rule out the witch slaughter explanation. Indeed, cannibalism has taken place at some point or another in many other cultures, whether it was due to starvation, criminal activity, or used as a means of social control. It could be that one particularly antisocial person engaged in cannibalism, and we should not condemn an entire group for the act of one person. However, there is one piece of evidence that is not explained by the witch slaughter theory. Resin from cooking pots was found on the bones. This definitively shows that the flesh was cooked, something that was not part of the witch slaughter ritual. Further, there are so many skeletal remains that have been treated like this, we cannot presume that it was a random criminal act, but that it was a quite significant occurrence.

I'd like to reiterate my point that the suggestion that cannibalism occurred among the Anasazi is not a direct attack on these people. We cannot, at this point, determine who ate whom. While the theory that it was a group of foreigners terrorizing the Anasazi people has not been proven, it is certainly a plausible explanation that does not tarnish our image of the Anasazi. Because cannibalism is so very taboo, even scientists are reluctant to consider evidence that points in that direction. However, science relies on objectivity, and in this case, the evidence is clear. Furthermore, the claim is not a direct implication of evil among the Anasazi.

Practice Test

W: The first and most fundamental step to take when studying an entity or phenomenon is to define it, right? Right. Starting with a definition ensures that there actually is something there to be studied and provides a certainty of what exactly it is being studied and, by extension, what is not being studied. Let's begin, then, by examining some of the aspects involved in the definition of society. A society involves a geographic area, like the United States or the world, for example, though a society can exist on a much smaller scale, like a local community. A society also involves a distinct identity. By this I mean that the individuals within the geographic area view themselves as a society. The people attending this university identify themselves as part of the student body here. Our common place of study gives us a common identity as members of this school. So, place is the first aspect we use to define a group — a social group. A big social group, we'll call a society. A society also involves a common government that sets and monitors rules under which the people in the society abide and coexist. At a national level, this is pretty easy to imagine. The society in any given country is under the rule of the national government. But there are also state governments, city governments, and our university even has a kind of governing body, doesn't it? As you might guess, things that we study in sociology are not always as cut-and-dry as you might think at first. So, going back to our definition of society, next we should talk about language. Members of a particular society share a common language through which they can communicate. It would be kind of hard for a society to function if its members couldn't communicate with each other. It is interesting to note that, in the US, we don't actually have an official national language. Most official business is conducted in English, so even though it's not the official language, it's the accepted common language here. And lastly, a society also shares common traditions, customs, and beliefs, though sociologists are beginning to question the accuracy and relevance of these last few aspects.

So, now that we have our definition, we can examine just what this force, society, actually does. For one, it organizes individuals into a system aimed at obtaining the things they need for survival. It does this by giving us guidelines for behavior, as mentioned in the definition. These guidelines serve two chief functions: first, they satisfy certain social needs, and second, they prevent conflict among the members of the society. Thus we have laws, some of which are unwritten taboos, that define and control relationships between women and men, adults and children, teachers and students, etc. In addition, we have laws against theft, violence, and other issues that could potentially create strife. Alright, with all of this in mind, I think we are ready to start thinking about society in a more systematic way.

Answer Key

Chapter 1

Skill A

Practice 1

01
Step 1
Correlation Studies: determine RELATIONSHIP BETWEEN two variables
- researcher doesn't MANIPULATE variables
- researchers MEASURE RATE at which variables change naturally

Relationship types:
- Y increases when X increases: POSITIVE CORRELATION
- Y decreases when X increases: NEGATIVE CORRELATION
- sometimes, a CAUSAL RELATIONSHIP can be inferred

Step 2
Main point: Correlation does NOT IMPLY causation
- cannot be certain because investigators don't MANIPULATE VARIABLES
- also, a THIRD VARIABLE may be affecting the correlation
- ex. Eating ice cream and drowning have a POSITIVE CORRELATION
- but a third variable is HOT WEATHER
- Correlations can SUGGEST causal relationships, but more RESEARCH is needed to prove it
- ex. A positive correlation between smoking and CANCER led to further research that proved a CAUSAL RELATIONSHIP

Step 3
Reading:
- Main Idea: Correlation studies can determine a connection between two variables.
- Supporting Idea: If the rate of one event increases when the rate of another event increases, they have a positive correlation.
- Supporting Idea: If the rate of one event decreases when the rate of another event increases, they have a negative correlation.

Lecture:
- Main Idea: Correlations found from correlation studies do not necessarily mean a causal relationship exists.

- Supporting Idea: Other, "third" variables may be affecting the relationship between the two variables in a correlation study.
- Supporting Idea: Correlations found from correlation studies can suggest the need for further study to discover if a causal relationship truly exists.

Step 4
CORRELATION STUDIES are useful tools because they describe relationships between different PHENOMENA as they occur in the natural world. It is important, though, that researchers be careful not to make the common erroneous assumption that a CORRELATION IMPLIES CAUSATION.

Correlations indicate when two VARIABLES are related naturally. This implies that researchers do not MANIPULATE either variable; they simply OBSERVE events as they occur. For this reason, it is IMPOSSIBLE to determine if one variable causes the other to change.

Furthermore, there is always the possibility of a THIRD VARIABLE causing both to change. To demonstrate, the lecturer states that there is a positive correlation between ice cream consumption and DROWNING. A POSITIVE correlation means that as one variable increases, so does the other. So, in this example, as ice cream consumption increases, the rate of drowning INCREASES as well. It is a FALLACY, though, to interpret these findings as indicating that ice cream consumption causes drowning. In this case, there is a third variable that is affecting both – the WEATHER.

Sometimes, it is ACCEPTABLE to infer from a correlation study that one variable affects the other, such as in the example in the reading of increased study time being correlated to HIGHER GRADES. It is very important, nonetheless, that one is careful to consider which VARIABLE affects which, and that there is not a THIRD VARIABLE affecting changes in both variables.

Practice 2

02 History
Step 1
Issue:　　- Historical REVISIONISM: A re-EXAMINATION of historical facts

Purpose: - Corrects historical IMBALANCES
               - Includes new INFORMATION
Motivation: - Despite scientific METHODOLOGY, historiography is BIASED
               - History is a NARRATIVE that favors the ELITE in society
Example / Argument:
               - Did Columbus DISCOVER America?
               - No. This is a EUROCENTRIC bias

Step 2
Key Issue: - Historical Revisionism has come to be used PEJORATIVELY
Why?   - Many HACKS and crackpots pose as revisionist HISTORIANS
               - They present badly RESEARCHED papers, books, and ARTICLES as fact
               - Their writing NEGATES specific events in history
               - They propagate a POLITICAL bias
This is dangerous. Why?
               - Non- EXPERTS are INFLUENCED to support an inaccurate perspective
Example: - Denial of the HOLOCAUST
Solution: - Legitimate researchers must COMBAT this trend by producing GENUINE research using verifiable DATA

Step 3
Reading:
- Main Idea: Historical Revisionism attempts to re-examine the past.
- Supporting Idea: Revisionism combats historical bias that favors the powerful.
- Supporting Idea: This helps correct existing imbalances in historical narratives.

Lecture:
- Main Idea: Revisionism is now often regarded in a negative light.
- Supporting Idea: Non-experts often present badly researched work as fact.
- Supporting Idea: Such work often reveals a political or ideological bias.

Step 4
In the reading, historical revisionism is presented in a POSITIVE light. The writer explains that revisionism is an attempt to correct IMBALANCES in biased versions of the past that EXCLUDE certain groups. The writer gives the example of the INDIGENOUS Americans that are ignored when historical texts refer to Columbus as having "discovered" America. The writer believes that REVISIONISM is necessary because as societies change, so do the power structures that govern them. Revisionism allows historians to include NEW information and re-examine the way history is written, so that it is told not exclusively from the perspective of the elite, POWERFUL ruling groups in a society.

The speaker warns us that there is a particular kind of historical revisionism that is very dangerous and negative. This form of revisionism is often practiced by individuals with no real SCIENTIFIC training or expertise. These self-proclaimed revisionists make use of CONSPIRACY theories and logical FALLACIES in their ill-researched writing on historical subjects. Such revision also often negates or DENIES that particular historical events, such as the HOLOCAUST, even took place. Their work influences non-experts negatively and gives legitimate historians a BAD name. Such revisionism must be COMBATED by authentic historians who use VERIFIABLE data and supportable documentation.

Practice 3

03 Astronomy
Step 1
Subject: How UNIVERSE was created.
Most DOMINANT theory: BIG BANG
Argument:
- Primeval ATOM exploded, flung MATTER in all DIRECTIONS
- All matter, LIGHT, and energy came from this
- HUBBLE found evidence to show universe is still EXPANDING
- "Cosmic background RADIATION" discovered — 1964

Step 2

Topic: 1. THEORETICAL holes in the Big Bang theory
2. ALTERNATIVE theories for how the universe originated

Argument:
- Big Bang evidence is too general and VAGUE
- Evidence also supports other MODELS
- Big Bang never proved beyond REASONABLE doubt
- Theory, therefore, remains HYPOTHESIS

EKPYROTIC scenario argues two parallel MEMBRANES of matter COLLIDED
- Supported by same EMPIRICAL data as Big Bang

Conclusion:
- Await new INFORMATION via technological advances

Step 3

Reading:
- Main Idea: The Big Bang theory states that the Universe was created when an atom exploded.
- Supporting Idea: Evidence of expanding universe supports this.
- Supporting Idea: Discovery of cosmic radiation supports this.

Lecture:
- Main Idea: There are theoretical holes in the Big Bang theory.
- Supporting Idea: The evidence is vague and also supports other theories.
- Supporting Idea: The Big Bang theory has never been proven.

Step 4

The reading explains that there is a POPULAR and dominant theory about how the UNIVERSE came into existence. It is called the Big BANG theory. This theory argues that the explosion of a primeval ATOM, BILLIONS of years ago, caused all light, matter, and ENERGY to form. The reading informs us that the Big Bang theory is SUPPORTED by Hubble's evidence indicating that the universe is EXPANDING. The theory is also supported by the discovery made by two scientists in 1964 of cosmic RADIATION existing in space.

The lecturer believes that there are many theoretical HOLES in the Big Bang theory. Actually, the theory has never been proven true beyond a REASONABLE doubt, and the evidence supporting it also supports other theories of how the universe may have been created. As an example, the lecturer mentions the EKPYROTIC scenario. This theory argues that the universe was created when two parallel MEMBRANES of space matter COLLIDED. This theory shares many elements of the Big Bang theory but also has some DIFFERENCES.

Practice 4

04 English Literature
Step 1

Issue: - Did SHAKESPEARE write the plays he is ACCREDITED with?

Answer:
- No. Some believe the Earl of OXFORD did
- Shakespeare is a PSEUDONYM

Argument:
- No CLASSICAL education
- UNFAMILIAR with aristocratic MANNERS/sports
- Oxford was nobleman and was WRITER
- Little documentation Shakespeare worked as ACTOR
- Extant SIGNATURES all DIFFERENT-looking, none on plays/poems

Step 2

Key Issue:
- Shakespeare AUTHORSHIP debate: Some SCHOLARS believe Edward De Vere wrote Shakespeare

Argument for Shakespeare:
- Little genuine SUPPORTABLE evidence for Earl of OXFORD
- It is SKETCHY, poorly-RESEARCHED conspiracy theory
- Plays not considered SERIOUS literature: reason for no name on play texts
- Numerous EXTANT documents refer to Shakespeare as actor and playwright
- Why would his contemporaries help nobleman? No MOTIVATION

Conclusion:
- SHAKESPEARE wrote the plays

Step 3

Reading:

- Main Idea: Oxford wrote Shakespeare's plays under a pseudonym.
- Supporting Idea: Shakespeare had no classical education and was unfamiliar with aristocratic manners and sports.
- Supporting Idea: Little documentation proves Shakespeare worked as an actor.

Lecture:

- Main Idea: Shakespeare wrote Shakespeare.
- Supporting Idea: The evidence supporting Oxford is sketchy and poorly researched.
- Supporting Idea: There is no motivation for Shakespeare's contemporaries to hide Oxford's identity.

Step 4

The reading claims that a NOBLEMAN called Edward De Vere, 17th Earl of OXFORD, actually wrote plays we accredit to William Shakespeare. He wrote them under a PSEUDONYM to protect his IDENTITY. The plays DISPLAY knowledge and information about aristocratic habits that Shakespeare wouldn't have been familiar with as a COMMONER. Oxford was a nobleman with such experiences, and he was also a WRITER. According to the reading, there is also little documentary proof that Shakespeare worked as an actor, and his extant signatures all look DIFFERENT, and none appear on his plays or poems. All this evidence indicates that Oxford wrote Shakespeare's plays.

The speaker argues that Shakespeare did write Shakespeare. He believes that arguments favoring the Earl of Oxford are poorly RESEARCHED and states that there is a lot of EXTANT documentation referring to Shakespeare as an ACTOR and playwright. The speaker also argues that Shakespeare's name does not appear on his plays and poems because plays weren't considered important or serious LITERATURE at that time. He believes Shakespeare's CONTEMPORARIES had no reason to help an aristocrat like Oxford hide his true identity and that, therefore, Shakespeare did write his own plays. He thinks the theory about Oxford is a CONSIPIRACY theory.

Skill B

Practice 1

Step 1

Main idea: One serious problem facing modern children is a lack of sleep.

Step 2

A. 1   B. 1

C. Sample answer: Receiving an inadequate amount of sleep is a serious problem for children today.

Step 3

Main idea: - sleep deprivation is ONE FACTOR in poor academic performance, but not the ONLY FACTOR

Other important factors:
  - NOURISHMENT (ex. breakfast) important factor
  - CLOTHING such as warm coats and shoes
  - home life; ex. FIGHTING between parents

Recommendation:
  - Educators must CONSIDER other variables before PRESCRIBING more sleep to students with LOW GRADES

Step 4

A. Sleep deprivation is one factor.
  synonyms: - deprivation — neglect, lack of
                   - factor — variable, aspect
  paraphrase: - Lack of sleep is one variable.

B. Educators must consider other variables.
  synonyms: - educators — teachers, instructors, professors
                   - consider — contemplate, take into account
  paraphrase: - Teachers must take other factors into account.

Step 5

A. 1. A child's DEVELOPMENT in school is LARGELY dependent on THE AMOUNT OF sleep he or she gets.

2. What is the SIGNIFICANCE of a DEFICIENCY of sleep IN RELATION TO other factors?

B. 1. The amount of sleep a child gets HAS A GREAT SIGNIFICANCE ON HIS OR HER PERFORMANCE IN SCHOOL.

2. With regard to other factors, WHAT EFFECT DOES A DEFICIT OF SLEEP HAVE?

Step 6

1. One problem that children face today is getting less than the recommended nine hours of sleep each night.

2. In addition to getting enough sleep, children need a healthy diet, suitable clothing, and a happy life at home.

Practice 2

Step 1

Main idea: An examination of history shows that non-violent means have not been as effective as violent means.

Step 2

A. 1　　B. 1

C. Sample answer: It can be seen from history that violence is an effective tool of social change.

Step 3

Key forms of non-violence are:

Civil Disobedience:
- INDIVIDUAL and government DON'T SUPPORT each other
- principle of "INDEPENDENCE" is the driving idea
- provides the MORAL advantage of being RIGHT

Passive Resistance:
- PEACEFULLY break the law
- must expect to be ATTACKED by AUTHORITIES
- should quietly RESIST without RETALIATION

Step 4

A. Principle of independence is the driving idea.

synonyms: - principle — concept, rule
- independence — self-reliance, self-sufficiency

paraphrase: - The concept of self-reliance is the main point.

B. Should quietly resist without retaliation.

synonyms: - resist — endure, defend
- retaliation — fight back

paraphrase: - Should quietly endure and not fight back.

Step 5

A. 1. INDEPENDENCE in mind and action is the guiding PRINCIPLE for ACHIEVING what is JUST.

2. Without RESORTING to HOSTILITY, Gandhi SUCCESSFULLY CONVINCED the English to ELIMINATE colonial GOVERNMENT in India.

B. 1. The guiding principle for ACHIEVING WHAT IS JUST IS INDEPENDENCE OF MIND AND ACTION.

2. Gandhi effectively persuaded the BRITISH, WITHOUT USING VIOLENCE, TO END COLONIAL GOVERNMENT IN INDIA.

Step 6

1. Although violent forms of protest are considered ineffective, Gandhi successfully achieved the independence of India without resorting to violence.

2. Achieving what is right and just can be possible through independence of mind and action, rather than carrying out revolution through violence.

Practice 3

Step 1

Main idea: Theories on alternative biochemistry suggest that non-carbon-based forms of life could be possible in unusual environments.

Step 2

A. 1　　B. 2

C. Sample answer: Some theories on alternative biochemistry contend that abnormal conditions could be home to non-carbon-based life forms.

Step 3

The argument against "carbon chauvinism"
- term DISCREDITS views that all life is CARBON BASED
- all current DATA indicate carbon is NECESSARY to life
- TERRESTRIAL LIFE is all carbon based
- we aren't able to test ALIEN ENVIRONMENTS
- we have no EMPIRICAL data about non-carbon BIOCHEMISTRIES
- PRESENT state of science not GUILTY of carbon chauvinism

Step 4

A. All current data indicate carbon is necessary to life.

    synonyms: - data — information
                 - necessary — essential

    paraphrase: - Carbon is essential to life according to current information.

B. Present state of science not guilty of carbon-chauvinism

    synonyms: - state — circumstance
                 - guilty — blame

    paraphrase: - Carbon chauvinism can't be blamed upon present scientific circumstances.

Step 5

A. 1. In fact, all ACTUAL scientific PROOF indicates that carbon is ESSENTIAL TO life as we UNDERSTAND it.
   2. The FUNDAMENTAL point today is that all CIRCUMSTANCES for biological life "as we know it" HAVE carbon in their MAKE-UP.

B. 1. That carbon is essential to LIFE AS WE KNOW IT IS A FACT SHOWN BY ALL ACTUAL SCIENTIFIC PROOF.
   2. That all circumstances for BIOLOGICAL LIFE HAVE CARBON IN THEIR MAKE-UP IS THE FUNDAMENTAL POINT BEING MADE TODAY.

Step 6

1. Although alternative biochemistry theories suggest non-carbon forms of life could be possible in unusual environments, in reality, such alien environments cannot be replicated or tested.

2. Despite the fact that the Earth is exceptionally silicon rich and carbon poor, it is carbon, not silicon, that has proven to be the successful life base on Earth.

Practice 4

Step 1

Main idea: Native American legal claims to the remains of Kennewick Man stand in the way of science.

Step 2

A. 2

B. 1

C. Sample answer: Native American groups are interfering with the progress of science by attempting to claim the Kennewick Man.

Step 3

Native American claims don't mean stopping the progress of science:
- Some SCIENTISTS take a HARD LINE
- Scientists argue Native American claims mean end of RESEARCH
- Native American groups not ANTI-SCIENCE, just want to be consulted or involved
- Science can PROCEED while RESPECTING Native American claims
- Many Native American groups involved in COLLABORATIVE projects
- Collaborative projects ENHANCE and clarify scientific RESULTS

Step 4

A. Scientists argue Native American claims mean end of research

    synonyms: - argue — claim, believe
                 - mean — represent, signify

    paraphrase: - Native American claims are believed by scientists to signify the end of research.

B. Science can proceed while respecting Native American claims

    synonyms: - proceed — continue, go on
                 - respecting — regarding, honoring

    paraphrase: - Native American claims can be honored while scientific study continues.

Step 5

A. 1. Respecting Native American CLAIMS to archaeological REMNANTS doesn't mean ENDING the ENDEAVORS of science.
    2. EFFORTS to freely CONTINUE science at the DETRIMENT of Native American BELIEFS are really the ROOT of the debate.

B. 1. Preventing the advancement OF SCIENCE DOESN'T RESULT FROM HONORING NATIVE AMERICAN CLAIMS TO ARCHAEOLOGICAL FINDINGS.
    2. The core of the conflict IS ENDEAVORS TO UNDERTAKE SCIENCE AT THE DETRIMENT OF NATIVE AMERICAN VALUES.

Step 6

1. The belief held by many scientists that scientific progress will be halted by honoring Native American beliefs and respecting their claims to the Kennewick Man is unfounded.
2. The raging debate surrounding the remains of the Kennewick Man shows that more collaborative efforts on both sides are required.

Skill C

Practice 1

Step 2

If I were so fortunate as to receive a piece of land, I would want to use it to do something positive that would not harm the land. Because I love plants and animals, and because I love nature, I would create a wildlife reserve. The survival of many woodland creatures is threatened because their natural habitats are being destroyed. I would want to create a place where these wild animals could live safely in a natural environment that is protected from development.

Not only would this reserve create a home for animals; it would also create an opportunity for people to see the animals in their natural habitats. I think that is much more enjoyable than seeing animals in zoos. While I would charge a small admission fee, the money would go toward the care of the animals. I would not wish to make a profit off of the wildlife reserve. It would make me happy to see the land put to good use.

Many land owners are selfish and see their land as a means of making money. They don't really care about the land; they only care about their investment. Some might sell the natural resources of the land, such as lumber. Others might build houses and develop the land in order to sell it later at a profit. Personally, if I had land handed to me for free, profit would be the last thing on my mind. I would take the opportunity to protect the land and all of the plants and animals on that land.

Step 3

1. If I were so fortunate as to receive a piece of land, I would want to use it to do something positive that would not harm the land.
2. Not only would this reserve create a home for animals; it would also create an opportunity for people to see the animals in their natural habitats.

Step 4

1. The writer of the essay prefers to use the land as a nature preserve rather than using it to earn a profit.
2. The writer states that he or she would use the land to create a wildlife reserve, which is an example of something positive that would not harm the land.
3. Yes, the writer points out that many people prefer to use land to make a profit by either selling natural resources or developing the land to sell for more money.
4. The main idea that the writer concludes with is that he or she would prefer to protect wildlife than earn a profit on his or her land.

Practice 2

Step 2

There are some types of decisions that require careful thought and other types that don't. For example, when I am at the supermarket trying to decide whether to buy orange juice or apple juice, I don't have to think very hard about it because it is not important. However, sometimes I make rash decisions about important things. When I make important decisions without thinking them through, I typically make the wrong choice. In my experience, it is always best to carefully consider my options when I make major life decisions. Major life decisions include career choices, relationship choices, and money choices. When I was offered a job overseas, for example, I considered many factors before accepting it. I thought about the location, the salary, and the possibilities for career advancement as well as being in a new culture and being away from my friends and family. In contrast, I have left a job without thinking about my decision. I once worked for an insurance firm, and I became angry with my boss. Without thinking, I quit my job. A day later, I realized that I should have thought that decision through. As you can see, in my experience, major decisions that are made on the spur of the moment tend to be mistakes.

I know people who prefer to go with their instincts when they make decisions. When I was considering buying a certain house, a friend of mine asked me, "how did you feel in the house? Would you be happy there?" The truth was, I loved the house, but I would have been foolish to buy it, because it probably wouldn't increase in value as much as some of my other options. Personally, I don't trust my instincts. I have to think about all of my important choices for a long time before I can make a final decision.

Step 3

1. In my experience, it is always best to carefully consider my options when I make major life decisions.
2. Major life decisions include career choices, relationship choices, and money choices.

Step 4

1. The writer takes the stance that it is better to think about important decisions carefully.
2. The writer tells about his or her experience of quitting his or her job without thinking carefully about the decision and later realizing that it was a mistake.
3. Yes, the writer gives an example of a friend who thought he or she should choose a house based on how he or she felt inside it.
4. The writer concludes that he or she prefers to think carefully before making important decisions.

Practice 3

Step 3
Suggested answers:
Keywords / key phrases:
engrossing, active, intimate, source of learning, interpretation
Keywords / key phrases:
exciting, stimuli, intense, convenient, social skills

Practice 4

Step 3
Suggested answers:
Keywords / key phrases:
information technology, relevance, practical, outdated, workforce
Keywords / key phrases:
creativity, anchor, indispensable, imagination, flexibility

Skill D

Thesis Statements

Step 1
Question 1: If my school received a gift of money, I believe the money would be best spent in hiring more teachers.

Question 2: Because of the multitude of interesting artifacts on display, I personally found my visit to the Museum of History and Anthropology while traveling through Mexico City to be a thoroughly enjoyable experience.

Question 3: I disagree with the contention that television has destroyed communication among friends and family; in fact, I believe the opposite to be true.

Question 4: Because of its many uses, including shelter and food, the maple tree is an important plant to the people of my country.

Step 2

Question 1: opinion
Sample thesis statement: I believe that the construction of a large shopping center would cause several serious problems for my neighborhood; therefore, I oppose this plan.

Question 2: experience
Sample thesis statement: From my experience, I have found that carefully planning my free-time activities provides me with the opportunity to get the most enjoyment out of life.

Question 3: experience
Sample thesis statement: There were numerous positive and negative aspects to my childhood in a big city.

Question 4: opinion
Sample thesis statement: Because communication is a larger part of daily life today than in the past, I believe that the ability to read and write is more important in our times than in past times.

Topic Sentences

Step 1

Question 1
(2) Having the Internet in my home allows me to communicate with people around the globe.
(1) The advent of the Internet is one twentieth-century change that has strongly affected my life.
(3) For instance, I send emails to friends, family, and work colleagues on a daily basis.

Question 2
(2) Many people radically change their lives after high school, so their means of future success should not be limited by what they achieved during those years.
(3) Many high school students, for example, may have difficulty because of health or relationship issues.
(1) In my opinion, some form of post-secondary education should be available to all students, not just top students.

Question 3
(1) In general, the Internet has not damaged my friends' and family's ability to communicate; however, it has negatively affected the social skills of one of my cousins.
(3) When I was visiting his house during the holidays, he spent all of New Year's Eve alone in his room playing *Doom*.
(2) He spends several hours each day playing online games and never comes out of his room to talk to others.

Question 4
(3) For instance, employees are more likely to work harder and take fewer breaks if they worry about their job status.
(1) I disagree with the argument that businesses should hire employees for their entire lives.
(2) Having workers who know that their employment can be terminated can help increase the company's productivity.

Vocabulary Review

Review 1

1. (B)	2. (D)	3. (A)
4. (A)	5. (D)	6. (C)
7. (C)	8. (D)	9. (A)
10. (A)	11. (C)	12. (A)
13. (B)	14. (D)	15. (C)
16. postulated	17. membranes	18. empirical
19. verify	20. precision	21. (D)
22. (C)	23. (A)	24. (E)
25. (B)		

Review 2

1. (D)	2. (A)	3. (D)
4. (D)	5. (A)	6. (C)
7. (B)	8. (A)	9. (B)
10. (D)	11. (C)	12. (A)
13. (A)	14. (C)	15. (B)
16. interacting	17. collaborative	18. foster
19. invariably	20. contend	21. initial
22. endow	23. require	24. technique
25. caution		

Chapter 2

Skill A

Practice 1

Step 1

When most people think of great military strategists, the names Alexander the Great, Julius Caesar, or Napoleon Bonaparte come to mind. <u>Spanish Conquistador Hernando Cortes, however, accomplished a feat that, arguably, outshines them all.</u> Around 1520, Cortes conquered the 5-million-strong Aztec empire with only 600 men, twenty horses, and ten small cannons.

In 1519, Cortes sailed from Spain to Mexico with 11 ships and landed at various points along the Mexican coast. He easily subdued the small coastal tribes at what are now Tabasco and Veracruz. These people told him of the vast wealth of the Aztecs who lived inland. <u>Cortes began to enlist the support of the smaller tribes</u> he conquered as he made his way inland, <u>a strategy that would serve him well.</u> <u>Since many of the tribes had no love for the Aztecs</u> due to the Aztec policy of demanding costly tribute from them, <u>they were often willing to join forces with Cortes.</u>

<u>Another circumstance that Cortes exploited was the fact that the Aztecs had a legend of a pale-skinned, bearded god, Quetzalcoatl, who they believed</u> had once taught them agriculture and who <u>would one day return to end their civilization.</u> Cortes was believed to be this god by some Aztec citizens, most notably, the emperor Motecuhzoma. Additionally, <u>the native Mexicans had never before seen horses, firearms, or the giant attack mastiffs the Spanish brought with them.</u> <u>Cortes exploited these two psychological advantages,</u> the legend of the light-skinned god and the spectacle of his horses, dogs, and cannons, <u>to conquer the entire Aztec empire</u> largely through fear and negotiation. <u>The brilliance of his approach leaves its mark,</u> for better or worse, <u>on the history of an entire nation today.</u>

Step 2

MALINTZIN was the secret to CORTES's success

1. Spaniards discover she can SPEAK BOTH NAHUA AND MAYAN and use her TO INTERPRET
2. Cortes uses her to win SUPPORT from the NON-AZTEC NATIONS
3. Unclear whether she was just an INTERPRETER or A LEADER as well
4. Independent SPANISH and MEXICAN sources attest to HER IMPORTANCE

Step 3

Reading
- Cortes was a brilliant military strategist
- Cortes was a great negotiator
- Cortes's brilliance changed Mexican history

Lecture
- Malintzin was the main source of Cortes's success
- It is not certain who the real negotiator was
- Sources lend equal importance to Malintzin

Step 4

The reading passage depicts Cortes as one of the greatest military strategists of all time and credits him with toppling an empire of millions with only 600 men and a few horses and cannons. **(1)** <u>Further/In addition to this</u>, it proposes he was a genius who exploited local politics, legends, and the spectacle of his small but advanced military to accomplish a nearly impossible feat. **(2)** <u>In contrast</u>, the speaker casts doubt on this version of history and credits Cortes's interpreter and concubine, Malintzin, as being the mastermind behind a significant part of his campaign. **(3)** <u>More specifically</u>, she asks us to ponder who was more likely the mastermind: the foreigner who had little to no knowledge of the politics, customs, or language, or the native who had knowledge of all of these and who was the one directly speaking with the leaders of the Aztecs and other nations. **(4)** <u>In addition to this/Further,</u> the speaker cites various sources, including accounts from Spanish soldiers and other conquistadors, as well as depictions in Nahua art, which support the case that Malintzin was much more than an interpreter and perhaps just as significant as Cortes himself.

Practice 2

Step 1

<u>The value of a professional sports team for a city's local economy is undeniable.</u> The benefits begin with the

construction of the stadium itself, <u>providing thousands of local construction jobs</u>. Once regular season play begins, an army of local workers is required to man the stadium facilities, for everything from concessions and ticket sales, to security and administration. <u>The economic benefits expand throughout the district of the stadium</u> as fans pour into the area from far and wide. These fans support local parking decks, restaurants, bars, shops, and often hotel facilities. <u>This contributes to the prosperity</u> of local businesses and provides a general boost to the overall property value.

<u>All of this revenue is of course taxed</u> by the municipal authorities. Combine this with the <u>millions of dollars in tax revenue that ticket sales can generate</u> over the life of a sports team, and we have a clear benefit for all members of the community.

These benefits are easy to see, but <u>the intangible benefits may be greater still</u>. A professional sports team with regularly televised broadcasts is often the hallmark of what people generally perceive as a "major" city. Thus, <u>the sports team becomes a kind of advertisement</u> for the significance and prosperity of the city itself, <u>attracting new business from the outside</u>.

Some may say that the costs of new sports stadiums are an undue burden on cities, but <u>all of the long-term benefits must be taken into account</u> before passing hasty judgment on the economic effects of professional sports franchises.

Step 2
Sports stadium not A GOOD INVESTMENT
1. Jobs created REPLACE other jobs or PAY LOW wages
2. Most money goes to MANAGERS AND PLAYERS
3. Tax revenue VERY SMALL compared to THE INVESTMENT
4. Team's BENEFIT to the city's IMAGE difficult to measure

Step 3
Reading
• Stadiums create jobs
• Stadiums produce tax revenue
• Boosts city's image

Lecture
• Does not create new jobs, takes money out of city
• Revenue gains are small compared to investment
• PR benefit is vague claim, funds better spent elsewhere

Step 4
The reading states that a sports team greatly benefits a city in a number of ways, **(1)** <u>while</u> the lecture says the benefits do not justify the initial investment, and that the sports team actually ends up taking money out of the community. The speaker implies that taxpayer money should not go to the stadium **(2)** <u>since</u> the sports team is a profit-seeking business, and they should not expect free money from the public. Further, the speaker argues that benefits such as jobs and tax revenues are not actually benefits if all relevant factors are taken into account, such as the kinds of jobs, and the comparison of the situation without the sports team. **(3)** <u>However</u>, the reading proposes that the benefit to the city's image is invaluable, ultimately attracting new residents and businesses and contributing to the city's long-term growth. **(4)** <u>In spite of</u> this fact, the speaker maintains that the city would benefit more from investing this money elsewhere, such as in education and infrastructure.

Practice 3
Step 1
In 1989, scientists in Utah made a controversial announcement. They claimed that they had carried out an experiment in which the results could only be explained by nuclear fusion. In their experiment, they filled a glass container with heavy water which had a small amount of salt dissolved in it. Into the container, they inserted two electrodes: one was platinum and one was palladium. The platinum electrode was connected to the positive charge of a car battery, while the platinum electrode was attached to the negative charge. <u>This process created an excess amount of heat—more than could be explained by chemical reactions. Because it could not be explained by chemical reactions, the researchers jumped to the conclusion that nuclear fusion was the cause. This phenomenon is referred to as "cold fusion".</u> It is not accepted by the scientific community, and it serves as an example of pseudo science.

The scientific method demands that a claim be subject to peer review. The validity of any claim is based on reproducibility. Because no one has ever been able to reproduce the results of the first claim of cold fusion, it has been rejected. More importantly, the data does not coincide with current theories of nuclear fusion. It is well accepted that, when nuclear fusion takes place, neutrons are emitted. For one thing, no extra neutrons were detected. Secondly, if the number of neutrons had have been emitted to support their claim, the researchers would have been killed. The only explanation for the experimenters' findings is that errors in measurement took place. This is supported by the fact that the methods they used to measure heat were highly specious.

Step 2
Cold fusion refers to a debatable claim that nuclear fusion can take place at room temperature.
- scientists must not dismiss observations that don't concur with current theory
- in time, scientists have reproduced the original findings
- measurement equipment has become more reliable

Step 3
Reading
- "Cold fusion" claims do not fit current nuclear fusion theories
- Scientists were unable to reproduce the results of the original experiment
- Positive results can only be explained as error

Lecture
- Science relies on reexamination of theories when evidence is presented to contradict them
- While results weren't reproduced immediately after the announcement, in time, scientists have reproduced the same results
- No skeptic has been able to identify an error that explains all positive results

Step 4
The debate surrounding the possibility of cold fusion, (1) that is, nuclear fusion occurring at room temperature, is centered on the scientific process. The reading attacks the scientists' interpretation of their results. When they found that excess heat was generated in an amount that could not be explained by chemical reactions, the scientists concluded that nuclear fusion was taking place. The reading states that because such an interpretation does not concur with current theory, it should not be accepted. The speaker points out, however, that science relies on continual review of theories. Observations should not be ignored (2) just because they are not explained by current theories. (3) With regards to the statement in the reading that scientists have never been able to replicate the original experimenters' results, the speaker states that in the years that have passed, some indeed have found similar results. In sum, the reading states that cold fusion claims have not stood up to the scientific process, (4) whereas the speaker asserts that the scientific community was hasty in dismissing the notion before sufficient time was allowed to complete an analysis using the scientific process.

Practice 4
Step 1
Recent claims that the ancient Anasazi peoples engaged in cannibalism are unfounded. The practice of cannibalism does not coincide with the culture of the Native Americans who are descended from these people, that is, the Pueblo peoples of the American Southwest. Cannibalism is considered by Native Americans to be one of the most evil acts a person can engage in. It seems improbable, then, that their ancestors ate human flesh ritualistically. The speculation that the Anasazi people were human flesh eaters is based on skeletal remains that were found to have been broken and burned. It can be demonstrated from these findings that flesh was removed from the bones, but that does not prove that the meat was actually ingested. A more plausible explanation, and one that coincides with the beliefs of the Pueblo peoples, is that these are the remains of suspected witches who were put to death. The custom was to kill the suspected witch by burning the body and tearing apart the remains in order to remove and destroy the witch's "evil" heart. his explains the broken bones and burn marks. It also explains why the corpse was ripped apart. While the

practice was brutal, it does not imply cannibalism. Any claim that the Anasazi people were cannibalistic is based not on fact, but on inference. The refusal of some to consider other plausible explanations is unscientific and irrational.

Step 2
Evidence supports the claim that cannibalism took place in Anasazi society.
- Evidence does not implicate anyone in particular
- Fossilized fecal matter proves ingestion took place
- Pot resin on bones rules out witch slaughter explanation

Step 3
Reading
- Evidence may be explained by witch slaughter
- It cannot be proven that human flesh was eaten
- Native American culture denounces cannibalism

Lecture
- Human carcasses were torn apart and cooked
- Fossilized feces and pot resin on bones prove that human flesh was cooked and eaten
- Evidence does not indicate who engaged in cannibalism

Step 4
The dispute concerning whether or not the Anasazi people engaged in cannibalism is based on evidence obtained from the examination of human remains. These remains show that human skeletons were torn apart, cooked, and had the flesh removed from them. The reading states that this does not necessarily imply that cannibalism took place. **(1)** <u>Instead</u>, they explain that these are the remains of suspected witches who were burned and had their bodies torn apart. The speaker, however, maintains that the evidence does suggest that ingestion took place. **(2)** <u>For example</u>, pot resin was found on the bones suggesting they were cooked. **(3)** <u>Furthermore</u>, fossilized fecal matter shows traces of human flesh. While the reading states that Native American culture would not condone such activities, the speaker maintains that the evidence does

not implicate anyone in particular in the act. She goes on to offer a plausible explanation that has been presented: that a group of foreigners engaged in cannibalism in order to terrorize the Anasazi. **(4)** <u>Thus</u>, the peaceful reputation of this culture need not be tarnished by the evidence of cannibalism.

Skill B

Practice 1

Step 2
Introduction: (C), (B), (D), (A)
Transitions: thus, finally

Body: (F), (C), (D), (A), (E), (B)
Transitions: by, also, in fact, as a result, furthermore

Conclusion: (E), (D), (B), (C), (A)
Transitions: because, consequently, clearly, instead of

Practice 2

Step 2
Introduction: (B), (A), (C)
Transitions: for this reason, in short

Body: (D), (B), (A), (E), (C)
Transitions: that is, while, however

Conclusion: (B), (D), (A), (C)
Transitions: further, in effect, therefore

Practice 3
Step 3
Introduction: (C), (A), (D), (B)
Transitions: for example, let us, in addition

Body: (E), (C), (B), (D), (A), (G), (F)
Transitions: to continue, in fact, in other words, to begin, second, first

Conclusion: (C), (D), (B), (A)
Transitions: thus, furthermore

Vocabulary Review

Review 1

1. (D)	2. (B)	3. (A)
4. (D)	5. (B)	6. (A)
7. (A)	8. (D)	9. (B)
10. (C)	11. (C)	12. (D)
13. (A)	14. (C)	15. (B)
16. (B)	17. (D)	18. (D)
19. (B)	20. (D)	21. (D)
22. (C)	23. (A)	24. (B)
25. (C)	26. (B)	27. (B)
28. (D)	29. (C)	30. (B)
31. strategist	32. campaigns	33. concubine
34. entourage	35. lingua franca	36. engaged in
37. ancestors	38. hierarchical	39. validate
40. plausible	41. undue	42. ingest
43. tarnish	44. condemn	45. welfare
46. (S)	47. (O)	48. (O)
49. (S)	50. (O)	

Review 2

1. (C)	2. (B)	3. (A)
4. (D)	5. (B)	6. (D)
7. (A)	8. (C)	9. (D)
10. (D)	11. (B)	12. (A)
13. (B)	14. (C)	15. (A)
16. (A)	17. (C)	18. (D)
19. (D)	20. (A)	21. (C)
22. (C)	23. (B)	24. (A)
25. (C)	26. (A)	27. (D)
28. (A)	29. (A)	30. (B)
31. tarnish	32. dynamic	33. pecuniary
34. welfare	35. remuneration	36. undertake
37. discourse	38. exempt	39. touchy
40. burden	41. up	42. in
43. into	44. on	45. top
46. (B)	47. (D)	48. (E)
49. (A)	50. (C)	

Chapter 3

Focus A - Verb Forms

Exercise 1

The reading introduces the idea of supply and demand. In particular, the passage explains that a person's salary depends on public demand for his or her talent. In other words, a person with a rare talent should earn more according to this model because supply is limited while demand is high. The professor gives several specific examples of this theory in action. First, she talks about ordinary people who make small salaries, such as bus drivers and fast-food workers. Then, she talks about people with special skills, and she points out that they earn significantly more per hour because of their skills. As extreme examples, the professor talks about movie stars and athletes. These people earn thousands or even hundreds of thousands of dollars per hour based on public demand for their rare talents.

I know a lot of people who treat their pets as family members. In fact, one of my close friends has had a cat since she was in elementary school. The cat is rather old now, but my friend takes good care of her. Actually, I think my friend spends too much time and money on her cat. Sometimes, I feel that she neglects her friends because she has to do something for her cat, such as feed it or take it to the veterinarian. In my opinion, it is unhealthy for people to focus so much attention on animals. If they focused this same energy and attention on people around them, it would make a world of difference. They could spend the money wasted on pet food and toys on more useful pursuits like treating their friends or donating to charities!

Exercise 2

The reading passage describes important space achievements in the 20th century, including NASA's lunar missions. In the lecture, the professor emphasizes the point that US astronauts are the only humans who have walked on the moon. He gives several interesting statistics related to lunar programs developed by other countries. In particular, the professor discusses Russia's lunar program. He points out that although Russia has sent rockets to the moon, no Russian cosmonauts were ever sent to land on the moon. He also mentions that China is developing plans to send humans to the moon, though those plans will not materialize for a long time.

In order to stay healthy, I walk whenever I can. This often means that I have to plan my day carefully so that I can leave enough time to get where I need to go. For example, if I take the subway to my university, it takes about thirty minutes to get from my apartment to my classroom. However, if I get off the subway one stop early in order to walk for exercise, it takes forty-five minutes to get to my classroom. Therefore, I have to leave my apartment fifteen minutes earlier than normal so that I can exercise for fifteen minutes by walking to class. By walking to class, I can also enjoy the added benefit of relaxing in the fresh air rather than being cramped and pushed around on the crowded subway.

Exercise 3

1. (B)	2. (A)	3. (A)
4. (B)	5. (C)	6. (A)
7. (A)	8. (B)	9. (C)
10. (A)	11. (B)	12. (A)
13. (B)	14. (C)	15. (A)
16. (B)		

Exercise 4

Both the reading and the lecture focus on the connection between poverty and single-parent families, in particular, families headed by women. The reading describes a government study that looked at all families headed by women across the US. This study concluded that the number of families headed by women below the poverty line decreased from 1960 until the present. The lecture discusses a similar study that found very different results. In the lecture, the professor says that researchers looked at only poor families headed by women. Between 1960 and the present, the number of poor families headed by women rose from 25 percent to over 50 percent. Thus, the professor correlates poverty to gender of household heads. In her words, the "feminization of poverty" is a reality in modern society.

It is often said that the <u>childhood</u> years are the most important years of one's life. However, I think a person's young adulthood years are more important than the childhood years. As a child, a person spends time either in school or simply playing with friends. School may teach the child information or even certain skills <u>necessary</u> for life, but I think these are generic experiences for just about everyone. When a person becomes a young adult, on the other hand, he or she can truly <u>individualize</u> himself or herself. In university, one has the <u>opportunity</u> to make decisions without direction from parents or teachers. Of course, the actions each person decides to take can have a <u>significant</u> impact on the course of the rest of his or her life, unlike decisions typically open to children.

Focus B - Sentence Formation

Exercise 1

1. The designation of an individual's class, which can be based on a number of different factors, <u>has</u> been of key interest to sociologists for decades.
2. <u>A child who is</u> only a few weeks old is capable of imitating a limited range of facial expressions that he or she observes from a care-giver. OR A <u>child only</u> a few weeks old is capable of imitating a limited range of facial expressions that he or she observes from a care-giver.
3. Children who grow up in single-parent households typically do worse in school than children <u>who</u> are from two-parent households.
4. Diana <u>Pearce, who</u> was an economist by <u>profession, suggested</u> a theory that proved popular among sociologists.
5. The female lion, <u>which</u> is distinguished from the male by the lack of a mane, does the hunting. OR The female <u>lion, distinguished</u> from the male by the lack of a mane, does the hunting.
6. A critical aspect of learning to read involves the integration of skills <u>that</u> develop at different stages of childhood, namely the ability to decipher sounds of a language and the ability to write.
7. One of the most influential theories related to cognitive development comes from <u>Piaget, who</u>

based his theory on observations of elementary-age children.
8. Paper <u>products that</u> are made with at least 60% recycled <u>fibers consume</u> 45% fewer raw materials than products made without recycled fibers.
9. The professor describes the Industrial Revolution as a <u>time when</u> great strides were made in science and technology.
10. A utopian society is one in <u>which</u> citizens live in perfect fairness and harmony with each other.
11. <u>Polaris, which can</u> be located easily on a clear night, is a reliable point in the sky to navigate by because it is located over the point of true north.
12. The claim that "laughter is the best medicine" <u>is</u> supported by research that shows laughter reduces stress, which contributes to a person's overall health and well-being.

Exercise 2

1. The bowl (that was) found in the cave was over 1,000 years old.
2. A child who knows he did something wrong will not look an adult in the eye.
3. Cats were important in ancient Egyptian culture, which flourished in the Nile River Valley for thousands of years.
4. The desk that was broken was removed from the classroom.
5. Columbus grew up in a large port city (that was) located on the coast of Italy.
6. The fossil was obviously a species of horse (that is) now extinct.
7. People who grow up near the border usually learn to speak two languages.
8. The legal age of adulthood, at which/when a person can purchase alcohol, is 21.
9. Snoopy, (who is) a famous cartoon dog, is a beagle.
10. Two critics who reviewed the book did not agree.
11. The university has recently changed its admission policy, which used to prohibit women from studying there.
12. By definition, sunrise is the time in the morning at which/when the sun first appears over the horizon.

Exercise 3

_IC_ 1. Musicians are only able to develop their technical skills through practice. Therefore, they must devote long hours to exercises that develop particular techniques.

_C_ 2.

_C_ 3.

_IC_ 4. Confucius did not begin teaching until very late in his life, but he had a lasting impact on generations long after his death.

_C_ 5.

_IC_ 6. In 1963, Martin Luther King, Jr. was put in jail for a short time, and that same year, his house was bombed.

_IC_ 7. Because young children are being exposed to violence and sexually explicit material on television, politicians are now debating a new law to censor some shows.

_C_ 8.

_IC_ 9. Most people recall that Narcissus turned into a flower; however, few remember what happened to his spurned lover, Echo.

_C_ 10.

_IC_ 11. The researcher studied groups of men from various cultures. Interestingly, he found that men's opinions were very similar across cultures.

_C_ 12.

Exercise 4

1. a. In the past, you would have to pay for a stamp to send a message to a friend, but today, you can send messages for free using email.
   b. In the past, you would have to pay for a stamp to send a message to a friend, whereas today, you can send messages for free using email.

2. a. Many airlines are offering discount tickets for flights, so more people are flying for weekend trips to scenic cities.
   b. Because many airlines are offering discount tickets for flights, more people are flying for weekend trips to scenic cities.

3. a. The architect built many famous structures, and he established a school of architecture in Arizona.
   b. The architect built many famous structures. Also, he established a school of architecture in Arizona.

4. a. Although my father did not hold a well-paying job, he enjoyed his job a lot.
   b. My father did not hold a well-paying job, but he enjoyed his job a lot.

5. a. The epic work follows the lives of forty characters through the revolution. Thus, readers often have trouble keeping track of who is who in the novel.
   b. The epic work follows the lives of forty characters through the revolution, so readers often have trouble keeping track of who is who in the novel.

6. a. A driver caught operating a vehicle while intoxicated will be issued a ticket. Additionally, the owner of the vehicle will receive a ticket as well.
   b. A driver caught operating a vehicle while intoxicated will be issued a ticket, and the owner of the vehicle will receive a ticket as well.

Exercise 5

1. Having been severely damaged by the storm, the building has to be torn down.
2. Having been left in the car on a hot day, the plastic melted and warped.
3. We are only able to objectively view the core of the problem after cutting through all of the media hype.
4. Wanting to attract more companies, the town will offer tax incentives to new businesses.
5. In the past, women were confined to the home by social pressure, being primarily expected to bear and raise children.

Exercise 6

_P_ 1. A student who waits until the last minute to study for an exam and completes assignments in a careless manner will do poorly in the class.

_P_ 2. Both by the way the couple dressed and by their interaction with each other, it was obvious they were on their honeymoon.

NP 3. Job opportunities <u>are increasing in fields related to Internet technology</u> but <u>have decreased in many traditional fields of engineering</u>. (are decreasing)

P 4. <u>Learning how to write Chinese</u> was harder for me than <u>learning how to speak it</u>.

P 5. My father taught me <u>how to drive in reverse</u> and <u>how to parallel park</u>.

NP 6. Shakespeare wrote <u>comedies</u>, <u>romances</u>, <u>tragedies</u>, and <u>plays based on real people from history</u>. (historical dramas)

P 7. She <u>spent hours wandering around different floors of the library</u>, <u>enjoying her solitude</u>, and <u>discovering old, interesting books</u>.

NP 8. Learning to write well is important for business majors because employees at all levels may be required to write reports that are <u>accurate</u> and <u>including important details</u>. (include)

Exercise 7

1. A child's voice is higher than an <u>adult</u>. (adult's)
2. Either a family learns to live within its budget or <u>will risk sinking into debt</u>. (risks sinking into debt)
3. I found most of the books required by the course interesting, informative, and <u>they entertained me</u>. (entertaining)
4. The violinist played with grace, <u>incredible dexterity</u>, and speed. (dexterity)
5. A shocking number of freshmen waste their first year of college not studying enough, <u>doing things harmful to their health</u>, and not utilizing the campus facilities available to them. (not taking care of their health)
6. In the art appreciation course, students will learn to analyze important elements of art and <u>recognizing styles of various art movements</u>. (to recognize styles of various art movements)

7. Most students expect three things out of university: to learn life skills, <u>meeting new friends</u>, and to prepare for their future careers. (to meet new friends)
8. The Hopi, the Navajo, and <u>Zuni</u> are three well-known Native American peoples of the southwest United States. (the Zuni)

Exercise 8

The reading and the lecture both describe Chomolunga, which <u>is</u> the mountain better known as Mt. Everest. The reading introduces just the basic facts about the mountain, such as its location, height, and <u>climate/ weather conditions</u>. The professor adds to this information <u>by talking</u> about all of the people who have tried to climb Mt. Everest. In particular, he explains that although thousands of people <u>have tried</u> to climb the mountain, only about 650 have succeeded. On top of that, 142 of those successful climbers died before they made it back down the mountain. Obviously, Mt. Everest is an incredible and dangerous mountain.

In my opinion, teamwork is a more valuable asset in a new employee than independence. Most jobs cannot be done <u>alone. Therefore, it</u> is necessary for employees to be able to work both with colleagues who work within the same company as well as with individuals or teams from other companies. Employees must have the necessary skills to communicate effectively with others as well as cooperate in forming strategies or solutions for workplace tasks and problems. Although an independent employee might be able to do certain tasks without help or input from others, these are not the most efficient workers <u>because</u> the tasks he or she undertakes are smaller or more limited in nature than the tasks which can <u>be undertaken</u> by teams.

Sample Responses

Task 1

The reading and the lecture define society in different ways. They both talk about groups of people, but the way each talks about groups is very different. In the reading passage, groups are categorized by size and type. For example, there are small social groups and large social groups, and both these small groups and large groups interact with each other. All of the small groups and large groups together make a supergroup, society.

In the lecture, the speaker does not define society in this way. Instead, she gives several common aspects that can be used to define society. Among these aspects, she lists a common place, a common government, a common language, and common traditions. According to the speaker, society is not necessarily a large supergroup. In her view, a relatively small group of individuals within a relatively small area can be defined as a society. She points to the student body of a university as an example. As long as the group of individuals has the aspects she lists, it can be considered a society.

Task 2

In life, a number of sources contribute to one's learning and development: parents, teachers, friends, television, books, and movies. Each source is essential to human development in some way. It is my belief, however, that parents are the best and most important teachers for a number of reasons.

First, parents are the first teachers that each individual encounters. Even before birth, mothers and fathers "teach" babies by talking and singing to them. After birth, parents teach by talking, reading, and introducing their children to the world around them. Scientists contend that children's brains grow rapidly between ages one and five — the period spent almost exclusively with Mom and Dad.

Second, parents teach children not only how to talk, read, and write, but also how to behave correctly. Infants, of course, do not know anything about other people. Parents instruct them how to be polite, how to show respect, how to handle emotions, whom to trust, and whom not to trust. In other words, they teach their children how to survive and thrive in society.

Third, and most important, parents teach by example. Because children spend so much time with their parents when they are young, they learn by observation and imitation. This can be both positive and negative. For example, children can learn harmful behaviors, like violence or smoking, if their parents exhibit such actions. Children, therefore, learn what they live. If their parents are kind, the children will be, too. If the parents are selfish, so will be the children.

The final aspect is the longevity of the relationship. Since parents act as teachers for 18 or more years before the child leaves home, they have a much stronger impact than a school teacher whom students may know for as little as one year. Indeed, even after graduating from university and starting a family of their own, children often turn to their parents for guidance.

Though there are numerous people and media through which children can learn, the lessons and examples received from parents shape personalities and influence lives the most. For these reasons, I think parents are the most important teachers in a person's life.